KT-524-896

MARY KENNEDY

Home Thoughts from the Heart

HACHETTE
BOOKS
IRELAND

First published in 2018 by Hachette Books Ireland

Copyright © Mary Kennedy, 2018

All rights reserved. No part of this publication may be reproduced, stored in a
retrieval system, or transmitted, in any form or by any means without the prior
written permission of the publisher, nor be otherwise circulated in any form of binding
or cover other than that in which it is published and without a similar condition
being imposed on the subsequent purchaser.

A CIP catalogue record for this title is available from the British Library

ISBN: 978 1 47366 697 9

Book design and typesetting: Anú Design, Tara
Printed in Italy by L.E.G.O. S.p.A

Food photography: Joanne Murphy; Food stylist: Chloe Chan;
Other photographs © Lucy Foster (Malawi; home garden, Inis Mór, cover);
Kerry Kennelly (Vesnova); David McClelland (formal wedding);
author's own collection.

Hachette Books Ireland policy is to use papers that are natural,
renewable and recyclable products and made from wood grown in sustainable forests.
The logging and manufacturing processes are expected to conform to the
environmental regulations of the country of origin.

Hachette Books Ireland
8 Castlecourt Centre
Castleknock
Dublin 15, Ireland

A division of Hachette UK Ltd
Carmelite House
50 Victoria Embankment
London EC4Y 0DZ

www.hachettebooksireland.ie

Leabharlann
7048953
Contae na Mídhe

WITHDRAWN FROM STOCK

Home Thoughts from the Heart

One of Ireland's best-loved broadcasters, Mary Kennedy's career in RTÉ has spanned more than three decades, including presenting the Eurovision Song Contest in 1995. She is co-presenter of Nationwide and author of the best-selling books *What Matters*, *Lines for Living*, *Paper Tigers*, and *Lines I Love*. A mum of four, she lives in Dublin.

For my sister Deirdre
and my brothers John and Tony,
remembering the home in which we grew up,
the values it gave us and
the people who made us.

Contents

The Roots of Home

'Just Home and Love! the words are small
Four letters unto each;
And yet you will not find in all
The wide and gracious range of speech
Two more so tenderly complete ...'

from 'Home and Love' by Robert William Service

When I first happened on those gentle words, my eyes lit up and my heart soared with delight. Robert Service, who was born in England in 1874 and died in France in 1958, had hit the nail on the head. He was singing my song. This was a man who travelled widely. He moved to Canada at the age of twenty-one and worked at many different jobs, often menial and back-breaking, before becoming a full-time poet and writer.

Service was known as 'The Bard of the Yukon' and is responsible for some well-known cowboy ballads, including the epic tale 'The Shooting of Dan McGrew', which my uncle recited from start to finish at Christmas parties when I was growing up in Clondalkin, in the suburbs of Dublin. Readers of my vintage will probably remember the story:

> 'A bunch of the boys were whooping it up
>   in the Malamute saloon;
> The kid that handles the music-box was hitting
>   a jag-time tune;
> Back of the bar, in a solo game, sat Dangerous
>   Dan McGrew,
> And watching his luck was his light-o'-love,
>   the lady that's known as Lou.'

As it happens, the lady known as Lou was also involved with a miner, who was not best pleased to realise that she was two-timing him. He appeared in the saloon to settle the score, 'like a man with a foot in the grave and scarcely the strength of a louse . . .'.

The miner might have appeared fragile but he was bent on revenge, and Service recounts the action in ten wonderful rhyming verses. As you can imagine, the story did not end well, and they did not live happily ever after. Shots were fired:

'Pitched on his head, and pumped full of lead,
     was Dangerous Dan McGrew,
While the man from the creeks lay clutched
     to the breast of the lady that's known as Lou.'

How did that happen? I hear you ask. The miner shot Dangerous Dan, but who shot the miner? Well, according to Robert Service – and he heard the story first hand, after all, in the bars of the Yukon during the Gold Rush:

'The woman that kissed him – and pinched his
     poke – was the lady that's known as Lou.'

Robert Service wrote other swashbuckling poems and stories, full of grime, blood and guts, yet he was responsible for the beautiful lines with which I began this foreword. They strike me as heartfelt and they encapsulate pretty well the essence of what I would like to achieve in this book.

Home and love are as important today as they obviously were when this poem was published more than a hundred years ago. I'm three years further along the road of life since my last book, *What Matters*, was published. There have been good times and bad on that road, and I firmly believe that what continues to make life meaningful for me is a sense of home and of love. If we have a solid foundation in those aspects of life, we have the means to grow, to thrive, to be ambitious and adventurous, to live our best life. Home is the launching pad, and love the rocket fuel that sets us on our way. Together, they make us 'tenderly complete' and give us the confidence to go out into the world in the knowledge that there are people who care, who want us to be happy and successful, people on whom we can rely in difficult times, a place to which we can return when life is hard. In American author John Howard Payne's words:

'To thee I'll return, overburdened with care;
The heart's dearest solace will shine on me there.'

I have a sense of home that has been fashioned by more than sixty years of living in different circumstances – growing up in the family home in Clondalkin; leaving at twenty-one to live and work in France, exposed to

Big day at number 31 – when a professional photographer came to the house, in 1962.

gut-wrenching homesickness; getting married and buying our first home; having a family; separating from my husband and buying a home alone. I hope that my varied experiences of home will permeate these pages as you and I journey through moments in time, contemplating life, how we live it, what makes it meaningful, happy, sad and, above all, real and authentic.

Like most people, I took my home totally for granted while I was growing up in a three-bed semi in Clondalkin, which, in the fifties, was the last outpost of Dublin on the west side surrounded by farms, fields and open spaces.

I love this photo, taken in 1965, at the front door of 31 St Brigid's Road, Clondalkin. I was ten years old, had just finished 4th class, and the long days of summer stretched out ahead.

My children, who grew up in a centrally heated home, laugh at the notion of my sister and I getting dressed under the bedcovers on winter mornings because it was so cold in the house before the fire was lit in the kitchen.

I don't think my brothers pursued the same morning habits. They were hardier creatures: our mother had to threaten all sorts of punishments to get them to wear hats and gloves on the coldest of days. Looking back with the hindsight of adulthood, I realise my parents struggled to pay bills, put food on the table and clothes on our backs. There were few extras.

Another reminiscence that draws peals of laughter from my four is the excitement we felt when six bottles of lemonade were brought into the house for Christmas. They were rationed over the whole of the Christmas period and we would each be given a glass, not a tumbler, mind, of lemonade every evening after tea when, as a family, we would sit down to watch television. I looked forward to that lemonade all day and would strive to make it last the whole evening. It was flat as a pancake by the time I emptied the glass but that was irrelevant. It was lemonade and a real treat. How things had changed by the time I was having my children. A two-litre bottle would disappear in one sitting when they were in their childhood prime.

My aunt, uncle and three cousins lived next door to us in Clondalkin. I loved when Auntie Eilish was minding us because they had a gas cooker and I preferred the taste of their toast. Uncle Tom drank coffee (from a jar!), and on Saturday mornings, I would bring my Delph tea set into their kitchen where he and I and my dolls would drink morning coffee together. Posh or what!

We came home from school every day for dinner, and I hated Mondays because the washing machine would have pride of place in the middle of the kitchen floor. The windows were steamed up by the sudsy water and it was quite claustrophobic, but I think it was more what we had for Monday's dinner that coloured my opinion of that day. It was invariably leftovers from

Holidays, with family and friends at Skerries. Mam and Dad are top left, and I'm squeezing John around the waist, bottom left.

Cousins together!
All family gatherings
were photo ops —
this one was taken
on a Sunday evening
in 1962 next door in
White's sitting room.

Mam (left) and Aunt Eilish with their growing broods.
Mam always got great value with my haircuts (top left)!

Studio shot. John's trousers and my skirt were both made by Mam. Check out my pudding bowl hairdo - also home made!

Sunday, plainly minced, no accoutrements other than mashed potato. Dessert was usually prunes and custard, my mother starting the week in a parentally responsible way. No need for Sir Bob and the Rats to ask me why I don't like Mondays!

I loved Friday because we had egg and chips for dinner, and any evening that Daddy was minding us we had a boiled egg for tea. I'm not sure that his culinary skills stretched much further but we didn't care. We were delighted with the egg and the bread cut into soldiers for dunking. Easy living!

The next generation of family beach pics.
Rosslare Strand, 1995.

Life was simple. We played tennis on the road using the tarmac markings to delineate the court. There were so few cars in Clondalkin in those days, that we could have a whole set played without moving to the kerb to let a car go past.

We went to Irish dancing classes and took the bus on a Saturday to elocution classes, all organised at great expense and inconvenience to give us poise, confidence, a sense of self.

It wasn't all a bed of roses, though. Back then all parents were strict, and disciplined each other's children when the need arose. Can you imagine that happening today? I don't think so. There were bullies who made life difficult as we grew up. I remember taking a different route around the village rather than pass certain people who would name-call or pull off your hat. Seems pretty harmless now compared to the awfulness of cyber-bullying, but it was horrible and humiliating, and to this day, I have no time for anyone who undermines another person, no matter what their age.

My upbringing at 31 Saint Brigid's Road made me the woman I am today. I was a shy child, hence the elocution lessons. When I walked I turned my toes in. Nothing like Irish dancing classes to rectify that! I was anxious and lacked confidence in my abilities to the extent that I would study for hours every day coming up to ... Leaving Cert, perhaps? Not a bit of it. When

Christmas or summer tests were looming, it was not unknown for me to put in six hours in my bedroom after school revising and revising. 'Nerd' wasn't a term we were familiar with in the sixties and seventies. 'Swot' was the word – and, boy, did I fit the bill.

The fact that I emerged eventually as a fairly together, competent, energetic and fun-loving woman is in large measure the result of home and love: the security of a family home with its routines and rules coupled with the discipline, opportunity and responsibility that defined the love my parents had for their four children. I am very grateful for my past. As Corrie ten Boom, the Dutch woman who helped many Jews escape the Holocaust, wrote, 'Memories are the key not to the past, but to the future.'

I am deeply grateful for the no-nonsense, no-frills upbringing I had in my family home. I remember every nook and cranny of the house, the garage and the garden. Recently I had the pleasure of being shown around number thirty-one by the couple who bought it after Mammy died.

It was my first time to cross the threshold in fifteen years and I was delighted with the changes the young family had made, extending, upgrading, breathing new life into what was, from the time it was built in the early fifties, a lively, busy, happy household. I was touched that Aideen and Tony had decided not to change some features of my former home, like the tiny built-in fridge

Lucy, myself and Eva on our visit back at number 31, Christmas Eve, 2017. The original fridge remains – kept as a memento – and it doesn't go down any further than the top of that couch!

that no longer works. I marvelled at the fact that it had serviced a family of six! The two hall cupboards, one on either side of the front door, are the same as they were in my day, even down to the small circular plastic door knobs. Mammy used to keep her photo albums in the one on the left, and the phone was on a high shelf in the other press.

That was where I spent hours in the evenings, perched on a stool, shivering with the cold by times, deep in conversation with friends with whom I had walked home from school a few hours previously. Obviously the

Leabharlann
2048953
Contae na Mídhe

night-time chats were of a different calibre altogether! The mottled glass-panelled hall door is still the same, and that was probably what moved me the most. I can see my mother and father opening that door wide, their faces warm and smiling, welcoming visitors to our home. There would have had to be a very good reason for me or my siblings to knock on the front door. There was a wicket gate in the garage door, through which we hopped and made our way into the house. Them were the rules!

The day when I revisited my family home as an adult opened my eyes to the solid rock it had provided me on which to grow, the launching pad it afforded me from which to move off into the world. The visit imbued me with a very real and deeply felt respect for my parents, who worked hard to give me that home and that love, interwoven to provide the basis for happy living. I consider it a tribute to them as parents and homemakers that I'm writing this book celebrating home and the many ways it manifests itself in our lives.

I am aware, of course, that home and love are by no means 'tenderly complete' for many people, a great sadness and injustice in this country. We all know of the hardship of some ten thousand people in Ireland who are homeless. That up to three thousand children will spend Christmas once again this year in temporary accommodation is just plain wrong. As Mahatma Gandhi said, 'The true measure of any society can be found in how it treats its most vulnerable members.'

I can only imagine the heartache of parents who cannot provide a home for their children. The lack of security, the feeling of being rudderless, must be horrendous. Every person has a right to belong, to have a place to call home. We are well accustomed to the joy and calm of a child who knows where they will sleep at night, who has a place to do homework, a table to sit around with family, a garden to invite friends to play. Without these bare necessities, children are at a disadvantage from the word go.

We are very lucky to have in our country remarkable men and women who are champions of homeless people and who dedicate their lives to alleviating the hurt and the hardship that these people endure on a daily basis. I have deep admiration for Father Peter McVerry, Sister Stan, Alice Leahy and others who take on the burden of homelessness and work tirelessly to provide support, compassion and love to those in need.

Another person who has dedicated her life to offering a sense of home and love to the vulnerable is Adi Roche. For more than thirty years she has worked with the children of Chernobyl, the infamous site of the world's worst nuclear disaster in 1986. I visited Vesnova in Belarus in 2017 and to say I was unprepared for what I witnessed is an understatement. I have travelled in some of the poorest

Adi Roche with Marsha, in Vesnova.

countries in Africa; I worked in Sri Lanka in the wake of the tsunami, and in Calcutta where five million people live on the streets, but nevertheless I was horrified by the awfulness of the area around the orphanage in Vesnova. The pervading colour is grey, the feeling is of cold and damp, the atmosphere of gloom and poverty. Chernobyl Children International, the charity Adi Roche heads up, has worked with the children in Vesnova Orphanage since the nuclear accident. The difference it has made to the lives of those children is phenomenal. And it's all about home.

Vesnova Children's Mental Asylum, to give it its official title, is one of three hundred institutions in Belarus where the state houses children and young adults with special needs who have no one to care for them. It's a grim prospect to the uninitiated yet it would be a lot worse if it weren't for the support it has received from Adi and her team over the past three decades. In some respects, it is a beacon of light in the area of state care.

The entrance is bright and cheerful, with painted corridors and light net curtains on the windows. The wards are arranged with rows of beds and cots, all bedecked with coloured duvets and pillows. Shelves are neatly stacked with clean bed linen and the children's clothes. Toothbrushes are lined up like soldiers in plastic containers, complete with name tags, on the bathroom walls. There are cuddly animals in the cots

The orphanage at Vesnova.

of children who cannot sit up, Duplo and other toys in the playroom for those who are mobile. All thanks to Adi Roche, Chernobyl Children International and the volunteers who travel from Ireland to bolster the hard-pressed local workforce and bring smiles, love and a sense of home to children who live with severe mental and physical difficulties, such as cerebral palsy, exposed organs, distorted limbs and hydrocephalus.

We arrived at bath time, and it took two people to lift four-year-old Ilya from his bed to the bathroom, one to carry his tiny body, the other to hold his enlarged head. The staff at Vesnova look after the children but offer few signs of affection or compassion. A lot of children have to be bathed, clothed and fed so there is little time for hugs and lullabies, except when a group of volunteers arrives from Ireland to lavish affection on the kids and to enhance their lives. The proof is in the beaming smiles that light the faces of those disadvantaged children.

Little Ilya responds so well to affection, singing and stroking. He smiles and, with his tiny finger, pulls down the skin on the lower lid that covers his eye, the better to see the person sitting by his cot, showing him love.

Vesnova is the most harrowing place I have ever been to, and my admiration for Adi Roche deepened during that visit. Her energy is boundless; her commitment to those unwanted, sick and abandoned children unwavering. She is the epitome of humanitarianism in action. What she has provided for those children and young adults is a home, a place where they are cared for and loved.

State law dictates that when a child reaches the age of eighteen they must leave the children's institution and move to an adult facility where the conditions are horrendous: they share cells with prisoners and are sometimes chained to beds because there is no one to attend to their needs. Adi has stepped into the breach with some innovative initiatives, including a number of independent-living homes in the grounds of Vesnova for young physically impaired adults.

I was deeply moved by the pride with which we were welcomed into one of the homes. There is a central living room, a kitchen, bathroom and bedrooms, each of which shows off the interests of its occupants. There are caring house-parents who look after them. They are the lucky ones in that they have avoided being sent to an adult institution. Needless to say, Adi's aim is to provide homes for more of Vesnova's children as they come of age.

Adi's organisation also runs Homes of Hope, which provides an alternative to state institutions. We all know that children thrive in a loving home environment, and to that end Chernobyl Children International has bought thirty houses in which they have placed families who care lovingly for their own children and up to ten previously institutionalised young people.

I visited three of these houses, which were all examples of love and home, tenderly complete, in action. The hospitality was incredible. If I was there yet, I wouldn't have finished eating all the cakes and other goodies I was offered. More importantly, the ease with which the children lived and laughed was uplifting, a joy to behold.

I returned from that visit to the Chernobyl area in awe of Adi and her team. She and others I mentioned earlier have made it their life's work to provide homes for people who need support, and when I contemplate the work of the Peter McVerry Trust, Focus Ireland, Threshold and other organisations, such as Chernobyl Children International, I realise that home has many manifestations, aspirations, possibilities and opportunities, some of which we hardly recognise as being dependent on and deriving from home.

I hope that in accompanying me through this book, we will emerge renewed in our appreciation of ways in which our sense of home permeates every aspect of our lives.

'But every house where Love abides,
And friendship is a guest,
Is surely home, and home-sweet-home;
For there the heart can rest.'

Henry Van Dyke

A Taste of Home

'I don't know what it is about food your mother makes for you, especially when it's something that anyone can make – pancakes, meatloaf, tuna salad – but it carries a certain taste of memory.'

Mitch Albom

And a definite taste of home, I would add to this quote. In *Tuesdays with Morrie*, Mitch Albom recounts time spent with a much-loved former teacher who was dying. It made him appreciate the important things in life: relationships, caring, time and, judging by the lines at the top of this chapter, memories. How often have you heard somebody refer to an apple tart as nice but not as good as the one Mammy used to make? Some mammies put the sliced apples straight onto the pastry base, others stew them to a pulp first. You either love cloves in an apple pie or you hate them. Your preference will often depend on the way your mother made hers.

I fall into the latter category because in our house the apple tarts were without cloves, full of stewed apples and topped with light-as-a-feather pastry.

Apple tarts were a treat at the weekend when I was growing up, but other dishes evoke memories of childhood and ground me in an appreciation of the comfort and security of home. I loved coming in from school for lunch on Friday because, it being a fast day, no meat allowed, we were guaranteed the egg and chips dinner I loved so much. Another of my mother's specialities was cheese soufflé at teatime. I still have the recipe she used, although my attempts to recreate the fluffy, cheesy, gooey dish have been less than successful. In fact, I could have marketed soufflés as an alternative to Polyfilla.

My sister Deirdre has made Mam's cheese soufflé with great success, and although I have eaten it at Deirdre's home on the Aran Islands, the first forkful transports me right back to winter nights in the kitchen at Saint Brigid's Road in Clondalkin, Daddy and us four children sitting around the table and Mammy taking the soufflé from the oven and spooning it onto our plates immediately, before the crispy fluffy dome could collapse. It was a comforting, tasty culinary delight for all of us. We would hoover up what was on our plates, then fight over who would scrape the bits off the sides of the brown earthenware dish that Mammy always used for that delicious soufflé.

It was definitely comfort food, although the term wasn't used at the time. Writing about it evokes warm memories of home and times past. If you ever decide to theme a dinner party around the swinging sixties, cheese soufflé will be *Top of the Pops*, a not-to-be-missed BBC programme that started in the sixties when I was ten years of age.

It's funny how memories can be so clear when triggered by food. When tea was finished and we'd washed up, we had half an hour of television before we finished off our homework and went to bed. On Thursdays, that half-hour was *Top of the Pops*. I wanted to be Sandie Shaw, tall (or so she looked on telly), with shiny, straight hair; barefoot, slim, exuding confidence and fun. This was the unabashed hero-worship of a freckle-faced, frizzy-haired, puppy-fat young one sitting in her school uniform on a hard chair watching from a Dublin suburb.

In honour of the lovely memories evoked for me by Mother's cheese soufflé, I offer you her recipe overleaf. I still have the spiral-bound copybook covered with patterned wipe-clean plastic in which Mam wrote her recipes. I'm transcribing it now, looking at her handwriting, remembering her and those simple times, growing up in Clondalkin.

Mammy's Cheese Soufflé

1 oz (25 g) butter
1 oz (25 g) flour
½ pint (275 ml) milk
pinch of salt and pepper
1 tsp mustard
3 eggs
3 oz (75 g) grated cheese
And this is the method, in my mother's own words.

Melt the butter, mix in the flour. Add the milk gradually, stirring all the time. When all the milk has been added, bring the sauce to the boil. Take off the heat and add the pepper, salt and mustard. Then separate the eggs. Add the egg yolks, one at a time, and beat well in. Stir in the grated cheese. Beat the egg whites till they are stiff and fold them gently into the mixture. Pour the mixture into a well-greased dish no more than two-thirds full. It's important to leave space at the top for the soufflé to soufflé! Bake for about thirty minutes at Regulo 3 (170°C).

Regulo means gas cooker, and I really don't know why Mam wrote that down because we never had a gas cooker! The soufflé should be golden and crispy on the top, soft and gooey in the middle. No pressure! Well worth the effort. The recipe finishes with the suggestion that it should be served with tomato ketchup. Pure sixties!

I can't think of a nicer tribute to home than to remember happy moments sharing food. As George Bernard Shaw said, 'There is no love sincerer than the love of food.'

There is love in the making and sharing of food. It's an expression of caring on the part of the cook and a feeling of being cared for on the part of those who eat. I have been very conscious of that from the time my children were born, and have never doubted the importance of cooking and food as a central part of the home experience. Modern living isn't an ally when it comes to this because of the demands of work, of commuting, of a seemingly unending schedule of extracurricular activities. It's not uncommon to hear now of families making a real effort to sit down to eat together at least once a week. It's not that long since it was the norm to eat together every day.

The table is where conversation happens, a few laughs, maybe silence, but easy silence. Sharing food is time out. We are present to each other in a way that doesn't happen at other times of the day. I have a friend who has a small basket into which everyone drops their phone before they sit down at the table to eat. What a good idea. It's impossible to avoid the phone if it's available. Something as simple as a query during a conversation as to the year, for example, Sandie Shaw won the Eurovision Song Contest with 'Puppet On A String', will probably trigger the response, 'I'll look it up.' Out comes the phone and the floodgates are open. The helpful looker-up will 'just check my messages' and then everyone else's hand slips into a back pocket: the dreaded mobiles are beeping. The people sharing the meal and the company of loved ones are now eating only in shared air space.

For the record, may I assure you that that query would not have been the cause of mobile sabotage around my kitchen table because, as a Sandie Shaw fan, I could have provided the answer off the top of my head. It was 1967, in Vienna. The song was written by Phil Coulter and Bill Martin. Would you like to know what she wore? A short shift dress. Unfortunately I can't tell you what colour it was because I was watching in black and white.

Cooking and sharing food has punctuated my life since my children were born. As babies, they were weaned on liquidised delights, the like of which no adult would countenance. Liver, carrot and potato took on tones of smudgy brown. Or how about broccoli, lamb chop and parsnip, or salmon, turnip and cabbage? I'll spare you those recipes. There are wonderful cookbooks with interesting baby recipes, much tastier than whatever I produced for mine. The combinations were dictated by my desire to introduce nutritious food at the earliest opportunity.

And it worked. Apart from Eoin, who survived through childhood on a diet of milk, bread and not a lot else, they all ate well. Eoin came into his own food-wise a little later. He's a tall, healthy, strong man, who likes cooking and eats well, although he still loves the milk. Open his fridge any day and there'll be several two-litre cartons.

All four of my children enjoy food from different parts of the world and like experimenting with different ingredients. Veganism and vegetarianism have become part of their culinary story, but more of that anon.

Maya Angelou wrote:

'I'm just someone who likes cooking and for whom sharing food is a form of expression.'

I couldn't agree more. Cooking for my family has always been an expression of my love for them. I'm touched by the many people who remember a piece I wrote about a little routine I adopted when I started working for *Nationwide*. That was in 2004 and they were still in school at the time, apart from Eva who had started at UCD. Some mornings I would have to leave the house very early to travel to distant parts for filming, so I would get up a little earlier and make a batch of simple fairy cakes, timing it so that they came out of the oven just as I was leaving the house.

I would arrange them on a pretty plate with a doily and leave the kitchen door open so that the smell would waft up the stairs and greet the children as they were getting ready for school and college. It gave me comfort as I was driving away to think of them coming into the kitchen to a batch of still warm fairy cakes for breakfast. I hope they felt the warmth of my love as they tucked in. The plate was always empty when I got home, a pleasing sight, I'm sure, for anyone who bakes.

In the intervening years, many people have remarked on that simple act and told me that they have adopted the practice. I'm delighted. Those little cakes are a symbol for me of the importance of staying connected to home, even when there are inevitable separations. I know every child would prefer to come into the kitchen and see their mother or father there to get them started on their day, but when that wasn't possible in my case, at least they came down to something I'd made for them with love.

My fairy-cake recipe is a pretty old one that I found in a Stork margarine cookery book, published in the eighties. Even though I have on my shelves far more visually attractive and innovative cookery books now, I have never thrown out the Stork books, partly because of the effort it took to get them. I was a teacher when they were 'all the rage', to use an expression of the day! There was a series of three and they were highly sought after. You had to collect a number of wrappers from Stork margarine and post them with your application. Can you imagine that happening today? I'm sure Health and Safety would have something to say about used margarine wrappers, albeit rinsed, being sent in the post.

I mentioned that I was teaching when these books were on the market: my colleagues and I used to share the wrappers. After all, how much margarine can you use over a given period? You needed three for each book, which makes a total of nine greasy wrappers if you wanted the full set. And I did!

The fairy-cake recipe is my go-to when someone is coming to my house for a cuppa. It takes minutes to throw the ingredients into the food processor and transfer the mixture to the paper cases in the baking tin. I put the cakes into the oven as the person is arriving at the house. By the time they have their coat off and the tea is made, the aroma of baking fills the kitchen as the oven door is opened and the fluffy fairy cakes emerge. They are also lovely iced. We have a tradition of making them when the family gathers to watch the GAA Championships and Eva ices them in blue and navy.

Last year, 2017, presented a dilemma. Dublin and Mayo met in the final and the kids, their partners and a few others were coming to watch the match. I made the fairy cakes and realised I didn't have blue or navy food colouring. In fact, the only two colours in the cupboard were red and green. My family was aghast when they saw the Mayo colours on their beloved fairy cakes in the centre of the dining-table. I explained to them that this was a gesture of magnanimity towards the other side, seeing that Dublin would undoubtedly win. Thankfully Dublin did win, although you'd have had a heart of stone not to feel sorry for Mayo as they came so close yet again, losing by a point. The family put their allegiance to one side during the course of the afternoon: the red and green fairy cakes were all eaten and everyone went home happy.

The fairy cakes have a life outside the home. I often bring them to the garage when I'm leaving my car in to be serviced and the lads eat them on their tea break. The cakes travel well and are still warm when I deliver them.

I have an almost unblemished record with fairy cakes. I had a recent disaster, though, that I shall admit to in the interests of balance and fairness. I work with a husband-and-wife camera crew in Waterford and, on occasion, Brian has been known to say when we arrive to a *Nationwide* shoot, 'So where are the fairy cakes?'

I decided one morning to make a batch and bring them along as a surprise. I was reminded of the days when I made them for the children before I left for work, except this time I had to bring them with me. I wanted them to be warm when I arrived in Waterford two hours later so as soon as they came out of the oven I wrapped them in tin foil. Not a good idea. They were hard and sunken in on themselves when I opened the package and looked awful. Suzie, Brian's wife, assured me they tasted lovely. They did not. They had no taste because they were dried up. They were still warm, though! Lesson learned. I still owe Brian a batch of fairy cakes.

Overleaf is my fairy-cake recipe, courtesy of the Stork book. I hope when you make them they will give you the same feeling of home, in all its comfort and ease, that they never fail to bring to my kitchen (recipe overleaf).

The American author and chef Julia Child, who died in 2004 at the age of ninety-two, was recognised as the person who brought the delights of French cooking to the United States, adapting the complexities of *la cuisine française* for a mainstream American audience. She was an authority on all aspects of cookery and passionate about food, so when she was quoted as saying, 'A party without cake is just a meeting', the culinary world paid attention. Cake is one of the joys of life and for too long it has been looked on as the devil incarnate by people not wanting to gain weight as they celebrate. A little of what you fancy is no harm. It would be interesting to compare the calories in cake and in Prosecco, which is *de rigueur* at almost every party. I like cake and Prosecco, which both add to a sense of occasion. Unfortunately,

I have no recipe for Prosecco so I'll stick with cake.

There's none of us isn't moved by the wonder and delight in a child's eyes when a cake with candles is produced to celebrate a birthday.

I have lovely memories of childhood parties with novelty cakes, made by yours truly. That Stork book was worth its weight in gold – well, gold margarine wrappers anyway. It had recipes for birthday cakes and, most importantly, diagrams to explain how to make them into different shapes. There was the rabbit cake, covered with coconut for the fur, and the Thomas the Tank Engine cake, for which the sponge mixture was cooked in two empty tomato cans, then assembled as an engine with a funnel on top. Eva was a big fan of Kylie Minogue, and I remember decorating a round sponge cake with chocolate icing and using a fork to make the ridges of a record, then placing a piece of cardboard in the middle with 'I Should Be So Lucky' written on it.

So simple, but it met with the approval of the Birthday Girl – and she recreated it recently when she made a chocolate biscuit cake to celebrate her cousin Dermot, a singer-songwriter, signing his first record deal. John and Eileen, his parents, had a surprise party for him in their house and Eva offered to make the cake. Needless to say, her centrepiece was one of Dermot's songs. I can't imagine the look on his face if it had been one of Kylie's hits! (Cont. page 46)

Fairy Cakes

5 oz (140 g) flour
1 tsp of baking powder
4 oz (110 g) caster sugar
4 oz (110 g) butter
2 eggs

For the optional icing topping:
7 oz (200 g) icing sugar
1 tbs boiling water
A squeeze of lemon juice to required consistency

My method couldn't be simpler. Preheat the oven to 180°C. Plug in the food processor. Bung all the ingredients in together and whizz until there's a nice fluffy mass in the blender. Divide this between baking cases and pop into the oven for twelve to fifteen minutes. Eat while hot with a nice cup of tea, and you'll think you've died and gone to heaven.

An optional extra is this simple icing topping (extra Brownie points with the kids!) – mix ingredients and spoon generously onto still-warm cakes. Top with a raspberry or blueberry for extra effect!

When Eva's cake was produced in my brother's kitchen I was warmly reminded of our birthday party for her twenty-five years ago, and all because of a cake.

Eva has become an accomplished cake-maker. When she and Benny got engaged she decided to make their wedding cake. I thought it was a huge undertaking but Eva put her mind to it and the end result was amazing. The family benefited from Eva's trial runs at the chocolate biscuit cake, and I was off the hook the Christmas after the engagement because Eva tried out a fruit-cake recipe. It was absolutely gorgeous and has now replaced my mother's recipe. Mam's was a loving reminder of our childhood Christmas in Clondalkin, of which her children have cherished memories. It was undoubtedly a busy time for her because the norm was to make three or four Christmas cakes and present them as gifts. For me, the excitement of Christmas began when I saw the cakes, iced, ribboned and lined up on the dining-room sideboard. That sideboard is now in my dining room and has been adorned with a single Christmas cake each year made to my mother's recipe. Now it's time for the new recipe to form part of our story, following the first wedding in the family. The texture and layers of flavour are rich and a little bit different. It's well worth trying. An Italian twist on a traditional cake.

Indulgent Hazelnut Christmas Cake

13 oz (375 g) sultanas
13 oz (375 g) raisins
11 oz (300 g) currants
9 oz (250 g) chopped prunes
9 fl oz (250 ml) Frangelico, plus two extra tablespoons
9 oz (250 g) butter
11 oz (300 g) dark brown sugar
1 tbs lime marmalade
6 eggs
3.5 oz (100 g) dark chocolate, melted
5 oz (150 g) chopped roasted hazelnuts
11 oz (300 g) plain flour
5 oz (150 g) self-raising flour
1 oz (30 g) cocoa powder

Can't you tell by reading the list of ingredients that the cake is well-named? Indulgent! The method is fairly similar to that for the more traditional Christmas cakes that we're used to making. We all know the drill. You've got to line the base and the sides of a 22 cm round cake tin to within an inch of its life, a job I hate. In fact, I've been known to leave the tin lined to use the next year to avoid having to cut and shape paper for the sides. The sultanas, raisins, currants and prunes soak overnight in the Frangelico (lucky them!). Cover the bowl in clingfilm so that the gorgeous liqueur scent doesn't escape. Next day, preheat the oven to 130°C. Beat together the butter, sugar and marmalade until pale and creamy. Lightly whisk the eggs and add them one at a time to the butter mixture, beating well after each addition so that they are thoroughly integrated. Stir the fruit and the liqueur into the butter mixture, with the melted chocolate, hazelnuts, flours and cocoa powder. Combine them well together. Spoon the mixture into the tin and bake in the oven for three hours. You can do the skewer test to see if the cake is ready: when it comes out clean, you're laughing. Brush the top of the cake with the extra Frangelico, cover it with foil and leave it in the tin to cool completely.

There were four tiers to Eva and Benny's wedding cake, two fruit and two chocolate biscuit, a recipe that Eva sourced in an Odlum's leaflet. It is an absolute show-stopper, sweet, unctuous and very popular. A finger is plenty but never enough! I cannot remember the number of times I've said I'll only have a tiny slice, then gone on to have several. The worst-case scenario is when the party is in our house and there's some chocolate-biscuit cake left over. I invariably have it for breakfast the following day. Not a good plan, but I can always find an excuse to justify the nibble or two that is pure indulgence.

Chocolate-Biscuit Cake

10 oz (275 g) butter
5 fl oz (150 ml) golden syrup
8 oz (225 g) chocolate, at least 60 per cent cocoa
7 oz (200 g) digestive biscuits, roughly crushed
7 oz (200 g) Rich Tea biscuits, also roughly crushed!
  (no mercy shown in this recipe)
1 packet of Maltesers, the chocolates with the less
  fattening centres (ha-ha!)
4.5 oz (125 g) walnuts, Brazil nuts or almonds (optional)
4.5 oz (125 g) sultanas, apricots or cherries (optional)

Eva doesn't use either nuts or fruit but she adds some small marshmallows and, if necessary, an extra dose of the chocolates with the less fattening centres.

Making the cake couldn't be simpler. You melt the butter, syrup and chocolate in a pan over a low heat, stirring so that they're all mixed together. Add the biscuits, Maltesers, and the fruit and/or nuts if you decide to use them. Then transfer the mixture to a 15cm round tin or a 2 lb (900 g) loaf tin that you have lined with a double layer of greaseproof paper. Leave it to get cold and set. Then eat. And remember: a finger of this cake is plenty but never enough!

Having read thus far you'd be forgiven for thinking we eat nothing but cake in our house. We have a more rounded diet than that, thankfully. Truth be told, if it was all about cake, we would be more rounded than is healthy.

It's no secret that I love to cook for friends and family, and because I am not in a relationship, I favour meals that can be prepared in advance. When I have people in for lunch or dinner I don't want to be running in and out of the kitchen and missing out on conversation. My friends are in my house so that we can chat, catch up and share the conviviality of eating together in informal circumstances. Here's Maya Angelou again: ' Eating is so intimate. It's very sensual. When you invite someone to sit at your table and you want to cook for them, you're inviting a person into your life.'

I have no desire to impress my guests with intricate, complicated dishes. The one-pot wonder ticks all the boxes. I have oodles of such recipes, and one of my favourites I got from a leaflet handed out in a supermarket a few years ago. Chicken fillets are marinated overnight in ten ingredients, then baked with some of the marinade poured over. The rest makes a tangy sauce, so good that I have been known to use a spoon to eat the last few drops. I serve this dish with rice or baby potatoes.

I always cook rice in a rice cooker. It's a no-brainer. You can forget about it and it cooks to perfection because, unlike me, the rice cooker knows when the rice is done. I always steam the potatoes. Likewise, I'm not a good judge of when they're cooked but the steamer is and they don't disintegrate into a soggy mess.

Home for me is a place for sharing with family and friends and is there a nicer way to do that than over a relaxed, no-fuss meal, like my supermarket-leaflet chicken? Try it. You won't be disappointed.

Chicken Fillets with Coriander and Lime

4 chicken fillets
5 fl oz (150 ml) olive oil
2 cloves garlic, chopped
4 tbs soy sauce
3 limes, quartered
2 tbs ground coriander
1 oz (25 g) fresh coriander, chopped
2.5 oz (75 g) ginger, chopped
a knob of butter
1 tbs light brown sugar
3 spring onions, chopped

Place all the ingredients in a bowl large enough to take the chicken fillets and give everything a good stir. Cover with clingfilm and leave overnight in the fridge. Cook the chicken in a roasting tin, covered with the marinade, at 180°C for twenty-five to thirty minutes. And don't forget to use up all the delicious marinade over the rice or the spuds when you're serving. Yummy!

Jay Leno, the American comedian, once said:

> 'Soup is just a way of screwing you out of a
> meal.'

I disagree. Soup is like a hug. It envelops you, warm and comforting. It's nourishing, cheap, easy to make and perfect for lunch on a cold winter's day. Another one-pot wonder that goes down a treat with almost everybody.

I have a couple of favourite soups that are always on the go during the winter. I make a batch and freeze what's left over, ready to put into the microwave to defrost on a Saturday when somebody calls by unexpectedly. A bowl of soup and a couple of slices of Neven Maguire's brown bread and you're laughing. This recipe is for his Multi Seed Wheaten Bread. It's in his *Home Chef* book and it's a winner every time. Neven's recipe is for two loaves so I have divided it in half. I wouldn't trust myself with two of these tasty breads!

Multi-Seed Wheaten Bread

8 oz (225 g) plain flour
8 oz (225 g) coarse wholemeal flour
2 oz (50 g) wheat bran
1 tsp bicarbonate of soda
1 tsp salt
2 oz (50 g) mixed seeds
1 oz (25 g) butter
1 tbs golden syrup
1 tbs Demerara sugar
1 pint (500 ml) buttermilk

Sift the flours, wheat bran, bicarbonate of soda and salt into a large bowl. Add all but one tablespoon of the seeds (reserve that amount for the top). Rub in the butter with your fingertips. Make a well in the centre of the dry ingredients and add the golden syrup, the sugar and the buttermilk. Mix gently until you have achieved a fairly wet, dropping consistency and make sure there are no pockets of flour remaining. Pour into a greased loaf tin and sprinkle the remaining seeds on top. Bake for about an hour at 180°C. Serve with butter and jam. (I added that bit of culinary advice myself!)

Our winters are often cold and damp, and I have always felt that a bowl of soup to welcome the family home is an expression of connection to the unit that brings us all together under the one roof. That connection is deeply felt also when you send them off to school or work with a flask of homemade soup. For me, there's a sense of satisfaction in knowing that what was made in the home is eaten in the workplace and provides a gratifying link to home and family. In the words of Louis P de Gouy, the French-born head chef at the Waldorf Astoria in New York for thirty years: 'Soup is the song of the hearth … and the home.'

My two absolute favourites that I make all the time are nourishing and cheap, cheaper in fact than soup bought in a can. One is Neven's roasted tomato and red pepper soup, which can be served hot in winter and cold in summer and which he includes in his family cookbook. The other is broccoli and almond soup, a recipe from my friend Anita, written on the back of an envelope with the indicator that you can leave out the almonds if you want it to be zero points. People who are watching their weight will understand the reference and be very glad of the recipe.

Broccoli and Almond Soup

1 large onion
2 heads broccoli, broken into florets
26 fl oz (750 ml) vegetable stock
salt and pepper
3.5 oz (100 g) ground almonds (unless you're on the
    weight-loss wagon!)
Dash of cream and a few pumpkin seeds, to serve,
    if desired

This is easy-peasy. You don't even have to chop the onion neatly into several hundred pieces, because you'll be blending it later on: rough is fine. Put some oil into a pot and sweat the onion till it's soft. Then add the broccoli florets, salt, pepper and stock, and simmer gently until the broccoli is soft. Blend it all together. You may need to add a bit more seasoning, or some water to get the consistency you like. At this point add the almonds, if you're using them. They add a lovely texture to the soup. Just saying!

I mentioned earlier that veganism and vegetarianism are part of our culinary story. Lucy adopted a vegan lifestyle while she was teaching in South Korea and has maintained it for five years. I have to say it was a struggle to find ingredients when she became vegan but now the selection is varied and easy to access. I wrote about this in *What Matters* and offered a few vegan recipes.

It's a new departure for my family certainly, but family gatherings always include vegan dishes now. It's often the case that the main course is vegan when the extended family comes together these days. Tom and Shona hosted a dinner to celebrate my birthday recently, complete with banners, balloons, Prosecco and a meat-free main course. It was delicious. I don't eat a lot of meat, although I'm not vegan or vegetarian, but I'm happy to enjoy veggie food for the taste, of course, but also because it embraces the diversity of my adult children's food choices and philosophies, and brings us together to celebrate a new culinary beginning.

One of my favourite vegan dishes comes from *Hello!* magazine. There's a wealth of good recipes at the back. So good that it's not uncommon for me to be sitting in the hairdresser's, feasting my eyes on the lovely houses and clothes of the rich and famous, only to be disappointed when I get to the back of the magazine and find that the recipes have been torn out. I know they must have been really tasty ones. This recipe for Vegetarian Chilli survived the cull – until I came along!

Vegetarian Chilli

olive oil

1 onion, finely chopped

2 cloves of garlic, chopped or grated

1 red chilli, chopped (de-seeded if, like me, you don't
like anything too spicy, food wise)

1 carrot, peeled and grated

1 courgette, peeled and grated

1 tsp ground turmeric

2 tsp ground coriander

2 tsp ground cumin

1 tsp ground cinnamon

2 tbs tomato purée

7 oz (200 g) cherry tomatoes, halved, or 1 x 400 g tin
tomatoes

13.5 fl oz (400 ml) vegetable stock

1 x 400 g tin kidney beans or chickpeas

salt and pepper

a good handful of chopped coriander leaves and sour
cream to serve

Fry the onion, garlic and chilli in the oil for two to three
minutes over a medium heat until they are softened.
Add the carrot and courgette and sauté for another two
minutes. Add the spices and cook gently for another

two minutes. A lot happens in twos here! Stir in the tomato purée and heat through before adding the cherry tomatoes. Pour in the vegetable stock, bring to the boil, then reduce the heat to a simmer. Cook for fifteen to twenty minutes to reduce and thicken the sauce, stirring frequently. Add the beans or chickpeas, salt and pepper, then cook for a further five minutes. A lot of ingredients, and the flavours are great. Don't forget the coriander leaves when you're serving your masterpiece. Serve with rice and if you want to add a bit of colour and cool things down, throw in a crisp green salad.

For me, food epitomises the nurturing aspect of home. I've been told I'm a feeder and I'm happy with that. I love to invite people to my home, to cook for loved ones, yet I can extract a taste of home when the invitation is extended to me and I'm eating in someone else's house.

I love brunch and had a most wonderful experience at my brother John's recently when he produced a meal of substance and variety, and it was only mid-morning. Two poached eggs on a bed of mashed avocado over sundried tomato pesto on sourdough bread. A veritable feast, washed down with pots of tea and eaten at the right time of day in terms of digestion. There's something really nice about making breakfast or brunch into a social occasion. The author and social commentator JB Priestley certainly thought so: 'We plan, we toil, we suffer – in the hope of what? A camel-load of idol's eyes? The title deeds of Radio City? The empire of Asia? A trip to the moon? No, no, no, no. Simply to wake up just in time to smell coffee and bacon and eggs.'

JB hit the nail on the head. The simple things in life are what really matter and they generally revolve around what we hold dear. For me, food and home are intertwined. Food facilitates social interaction, which is life-enhancing and provides the sense of belonging and security we all crave that allow us to thrive as living, loving beings. I can't think of a better way to end this chapter than with the words of Charles Simic, the Pulitzer Prize-winning Serbian-American poet: 'When our souls are happy, they talk about food.'

Home and Away

'Rain is grace; rain is the sky condescending to the earth;
without rain, there would be no life.'

John Updike

At half past three on a Tuesday afternoon in April, the plane touched down in Chileka airport in Blantyre, in the south of Malawi. Everyone in our group of seventeen was eager to disembark. We wanted to smell the fresh African air, to feel the sun on our backs, to stretch our limbs after twenty hours of non-stop cramped travel in full-to-capacity aircraft from Dublin to Addis Ababa, then on to Llilongwe and finally to Blantyre in the south of Malawi. We were at the start of our ten-day adventure in the country that is known around the world as 'the warm heart of Africa'.

Can't you just sense the excitement and anticipation as you read this? Well, erase that thought because to say that our adventure began on a damp note is to underestimate the ferocity of the deluge that greeted us as we landed. My heart sank as I looked out of the window and saw the rain hopping off the runway. It was like a scene from the 1999 movie version of *Angela's Ashes* where it seemed that every time somebody put their nose outside the door the heavens opened. Really they should have considered gathering up the animals two by two and building an ark!

The rain was so heavy in Blantyre as we arrived that the pilot announced we could not leave the aircraft until it eased. Picture the scene. Disembarking passengers with their carry-on luggage lining up in the aisles alongside

others, still seated, eager to continue their onward journey and make their connecting flight after they've got rid of us. Can't you just feel the loving vibe? It's cramped, it's muggy and it's lashing rain outside. Forgive me if I'm wrong but I do not know any Irish person who goes to Africa wanting anything other than respite from the grey skies and incessant rain that are the bane of our lives at home. And I'm certainly one of those true blue Irish people. That day, to me, rain was not grace.

When the torrent eventually abated to a lesser torrent, we were allowed to leave the plane and head via passport control, and the payment of an unanticipated seventy-five dollars for a visa, to the bus that would take us to our first overnight stop: a lodge in a wildlife park on the outskirts of Blantyre. By now it was dark, still raining and cold. As I unpacked and looked at the clothes I had brought, the thought entered my head that I would probably have to wear every single stitch at the same time to stay warm. Nothing like a hot shower, though, to shake off the dust and travails of the day. The shower was indeed hot and very welcome until the power went and I was left in the dark lamenting that I hadn't unpacked the torch we were advised to bring along in case of just this scenario.

It was the last straw. From the moment, earlier that afternoon, when I had contemplated, with a sinking heart, the little bit of the runway I could see through the porthole of the plane, with the rain hopping off the tarmac, through to the bus journey in the rain, finally alighting to cold air and now no electricity, I was reminded, yet again, how much my mood is affected by the weather. Negative thoughts began to creep into my head, and the uncertainty and anxiety that are no strangers to me reared their ugly little heads.

'This trip was a mistake'; 'I should have stayed closer to home'; 'Story of my life'; 'I can't wait to go home.' I was feeling sorry for myself big-time, but as I write these lines now I feel embarrassed by such selfish and self-absorbed notions and feel disappointed in myself that I had let them infiltrate in that way. Isn't it a pity that our thoughts and feelings can hold so many of us to ransom and dictate the way we are in a particular moment? I certainly fall into that category and have great admiration for people who can rise above those moments and remain positive when disappointment visits, like several members of our group. They were unfazed by the rain, remained good-humoured and upbeat despite their obvious disappointment on arrival for a much-anticipated ten days under African skies.

When I look back on that moment now, I see it in a totally different light. For a start, as we were travelling through the rain in a covered bus from the airport to our lodgings, the good people of Blantyre were making their way on foot along the crowded streets of the city.

Some had umbrellas, most did not. I noticed a young boy, soaked to the skin, making his way home from school barefoot. He was carrying his shoes, probably in an effort to keep them dry for the following day. Groups of women, also soaked to the skin, crouched on the sides of the road, selling vegetables and household goods. Most of the homes along the way had mud walls with corrugated-iron roofs, which would have been unable to withstand the heavy rain. The families would have had a miserable, damp night. And there was me feeling sorry for myself because the power had failed while I was in the shower.

I remember, on a previous visit to Africa, spending a night in a very remote part of Kenya when the winds began to rise: a storm was brewing. This was at the end of a two-week visit during which the sun had shone hot every day. The prospect of a storm was exciting, a bit of a novelty. The rains when they came were unrelenting throughout the night. I was with two friends from Ireland and we were staying with a priest from Cork. A proud Corkman, for sure. He had painted the perimeter stones of his little garden in red and white. A reminder of home so far away and so different from the place where he was living, ministering to people who had very little compared to the material comforts we take for granted in our part of the world.

Right through the night the rain pelted off the

corrugated roof of my bedroom. I was glad to be indoors, tucked up and cosy in my bed, totally unaware of what the night was like for the people in the village. Until the following morning. The storm passed over at around six a.m., in time for Mass at seven in the church adjoining Father Ollie's house. On arrival there, we were greeted by a congregation that had obviously spent a night of misery in homes that were totally inadequate to provide shelter from a storm. I was sitting behind two young boys, aged about ten, who were literally shivering in their wet T-shirts and shorts. That scenario was repeated throughout the little chapel, and when I mentioned it to Father Ollie, he assured me that they would have had a wet and sleepless night but that they welcomed any drop of rain in this arid part of the country.

'Remember that every drop of rain that falls bears into the bosom of the earth a quality of beautiful fertility.' I'm sure those words of the English philosopher George Henry Lewes, best known as the partner and soulmate of the novelist George Eliot, would have the people of Father Ollie's parish in Turkana nodding in agreement.

The same is true of the people of Malawi certainly. They endure the discomfort of the rain pouring into their homes, leaving them cold and shivering, and disturbing their night's sleep for two reasons. First, they have no choice because their houses are simple structures of mud or, if they're lucky, porous block walls, and either

A lovely moment, being welcomed into a family home in Nangoma.

thatched or corrugated roofs. Second, their livelihood depends on the soil and what they can grow so the rains when they come are a welcome ally.

Following that inauspicious start to the visit, the rain was non-existent until we arrived back in Blantyre on our homeward journey. Note to self: avoid Blantyre next time! By that stage I didn't mind. I was focused on returning home and had enjoyed ten days that were interesting, rewarding, and very special: I was accompanied by my daughter Lucy, a young woman of strong character, imbued with a sense of adventure, creativity – she took many of the photographs that appear in this book – conscience and commitment.

Readers of my previous books will know that Lucy is the youngest of my four children, and that I felt my heart would break when, at the age of twenty-one, having graduated from UCD with a social-science degree, she left Ireland to teach English in South Korea for two years. I will never forget the stomach-churning feeling of seeing her go through the security gate at Dublin Airport on the day of her departure, the tears that flowed until I could cry no more and the devastation of returning home, going into her bedroom and seeing empty hangers in her wardrobe.

Lucy spent two wonderful years in Korea. I visited her during her first year and was a very proud mammy when the principal of her school spoke of her in glowing terms. She was a conscientious teacher, the children loved her, and they were very sad when she decided to move to Australia to continue the adventure.

Although I missed Lucy terribly while she was away, I realised this was a great opportunity and I encouraged her to make the most of it. I believe the experience of living in another culture is invaluable, a rich learning curve that not only broadens your outlook on the world but provides a genuine appreciation of home and family. We have to move outside what's familiar to truly appreciate its place in our lives. After I graduated back in the seventies I went to France to teach English. The experience opened my eyes to the importance of my family, with its unconditional love, and my home, full of comfort, joy and, of course, limitations. It was the seventies after all!

France awakened me to a brave new world of freedom, a language and culture with which I fell in love and still adore, and endless culinary possibilities. When I went home for a holiday I was determined to introduce my family to *salade à la française* so I set about making a vinaigrette. This was not a successful endeavour. For a start, the only place I could buy olive oil back then was in Mr Shield's chemist shop at the top of St Brigid's Road where we lived. As for wine vinegar, forget it. Vinegar was what you got on your chips from the Roma Café on Tower Road!

Come to think of it, salads were quite a different animal in Ireland from those I had grown to love in France. We had them often for tea on Sundays. You lined the plate with lettuce leaves, placed two slices of rolled-up cooked ham in the centre and surrounded it with sliced tomato, half a hard-boiled egg, a few pickled onions and perhaps a scoop of potato salad. Suffice it to say my green salad with vinaigrette made from Mr Shield's olive oil and malt vinegar was not a big hit with the Kennedy family. I think they yearned for the salad cream that we placed in large dollops on the Sunday teatime salads!

I have encountered many variations of French dressings in the intervening years and I think my favourite is a mix of a few of them:

French Dressing

6 dessertspoons olive oil
3 to 4 dessertspoons balsamic vinegar
(I tend to use 4 because I like it to be quite tart)
1 to 2 cloves of crushed garlic
(I use 2. Guess why? I like it to be quite garlicky!)
1 tsp honey
1 tsp brown sugar
1 tsp of Dijon mustard
a few drops of lemon juice
pinch of salt and pepper

Put all the ingredients into a screw top jar and shake, shake, shake. Pour over your salad and simply toss, toss, toss. It's a nice mix of tart and sweet flavours and keeps for about a week in the fridge.

Every time I make a vinaigrette, which is often, I remember with fondness the year I spent teaching English in the Université de Haute-Bretagne. I was a naïve twenty-one-year-old when I embarked on that adventure and it was one of the best things I've ever done. I learned so much about myself while my eyes were opened to different people and a very different culture. I experienced terrible homesickness at the beginning. My heart ached for all the familiar simple things of home. I missed my parents, my bedroom, my friends.

It was hard to find a place to live, but after a lonely two weeks in an empty, soulless university residence, I rented a one-room studio apartment in a quaint old building with mice coming out to play during the night. Mind you, the mice weren't the only ones who came out to play at night. I realised before too long that I was living in the red-light district of Rennes. I moved out quickly and ended up sharing an apartment with a Scottish girl, who became a lifelong friend. All's well that ends well.

I had a stimulating, interesting year and was definitely bitten by the travel bug as a result. I was also infused with an appreciation of home and a realisation that, 'No matter how simple, there's no place like home!'

I love visiting other people's homes in different parts of the world and comparing their living experiences with my own. I appreciate the differences and the similarities, and know that a secure and nurturing home can launch a person on a lifelong adventure of travel, education and exploration, full of confidence, secure in the knowledge that there is a safe harbour to which they can always return.

*La belle France —
as an au pair on
the Côte d'Azur*

Living the life in Brittany after graduation.

勤政殿

Matching sunnies at
Gyeongbokgung, Seoul.

The similarities between my experience and Lucy's are uncanny. She also was twenty-one when she decided she'd like to travel. She also had difficulty finding an apartment and ended up living in a small rural town that was quite a commute from her school. Every morning she walked twenty minutes to the station and, after a half-hour train journey, walked another half-hour to get to her school in a newly built satellite town outside Sejong. Needless to say, she repeated the journey at the end of the day.

Lucy spent her second year in Korea teaching in a primary school in Daegu where her apartment was just a five-minute walk from the school. Bliss! Especially after a year of the 6.30 a.m. starts. As Nietzsche said, 'That which does not kill us makes us stronger.'

Lucy emerged from her two years in Korea as a mature young woman of conviction, passion and principles. She certainly has the courage of those convictions and she sticks by those principles. She cares deeply about the planet and has never wavered from the veganism which she embraced in Korea.

Like mother, like daughter applies with regard to wanderlust. Lucy used her time in Korea to travel in the area. She explored South Korea extensively, spent time in Vietnam and Japan, and since her return, she has holidayed in China. When Lucy decided she would like to make a career as a photographer, she set about realising that dream in a conscientious, determined way, honing her skills in lots of different settings, gaining much experience and knowledge.

It was a real privilege to travel to Africa with my daughter. It felt like an extension of home, an addition to the relationship we have as mother and daughter in Ireland. I enjoyed just being in Lucy's company from

Lucy with some of the local children and, opposite, young boys show off their makeshift football.

morning till night, removed from the constraints of working life in Ireland. We shared the tasks of making sure we had enough water, sunscreen and mosquito spray, and of tucking in the mosquito nets last thing at night. It was exhilarating to have music playing in the room as we showered and got ready for the day, something I would never think of but Lucy provided it on her phone first thing every morning.

We'd been in Malawi a week, and had shared some really lovely moments, when we went for a walk outside our lodgings in a remote area around Lake Malawi. Lucy wanted to take pictures and we met some small

Children of Nangoma.

groups of children walking along the way. It was a special moment for me as a mother to witness how gentle and respectful Lucy was with those little ones. We do our best to rear our children to be caring and kind, and we worry constantly about our skills as parents, so it's lovely when we get an opportunity to see them demonstrating the values they've been taught.

I savoured the moment as I watched Lucy crouch to chat with the children, laugh with the exuberant ones and speak gently with the shy ones, and I allowed myself an imaginary pat on the back.

It's six thirty a.m. on Easter Sunday and I'm writing this in bed in Ngoza Lodge right in the heart of a bustling African village. There's a wooden beam separating my bed from Lucy's and she is fast asleep under her mosquito net. We're staying in very basic one-roomed cottages. A curtain separates the toilet from the bedroom, with a sink and a shower in the room, and the all-important mosquito nets envelop the little single beds. The village is on the shores of Lake Malawi so this is mosquito country.

As I look out through the windows, which are covered with mesh (there's no need for glass, just something to keep the mozzies out), I see young boys and girls filling large brightly coloured buckets with water from the lake. They are already about their early-morning chores, laughing and chatting. Once the buckets are filled, they place them on their heads and make their way back to their homes. Normally it's the women who perform this task but the children are on school holidays so they can help out.

The women are at the water's edge also, washing clothes, and one is bathing her baby. I don't imagine there will be any Easter egg hunts around the village today. The jobs of fetching and carrying, cooking and washing will continue as every other day. The children will play in the streets and be alert to any foreigners who may be passing. They love to have their photographs taken and to see themselves in the picture. It's a novelty

Women washing clothes at the river's edge.

and exciting for them to see their image. Unlike in our part of the world, they are not seeing themselves in mirrors every day. Sometimes when you take a picture of a group you have to point out to its members who is who because they do not know what they look like.

Lucy, at twenty-five, is the youngest member of our group of seventeen. There's another young woman in her twenties and the remaining fifteen of us won't see fifty again. About half of us won't receive another sixtieth-birthday card. There's a great mix of people from various walks of life, all good fun and mindful of each other. Lucy is enjoying the company and the lighthearted irreverence that often accompanies ageing. It's refreshing in a world that seems obsessed with youth and the body beautiful. As her mother, I'm delighted and even a little bit proud (in a good way!) of how she's mingling and at the centre of things.

Some of the women swim daily in Ireland and do a skinny-dip here from time to time to raise funds for the Sunergy projects we have come to visit. Their stories

about those swims, their feelings about stripping off and people's reactions to them, have been greeted with howls of laughter. These are women with big personalities, big hearts and a wonderful sense of humour. Lucy has relished their company and they hers. Just as travel broadens the mind and affects one's outlook on life, I believe that time with older people opens the minds of the young to the richness of different personalities and the struggles that people overcome.

Lucy has absorbed and become part of the life stories she has heard on this trip. She has expressed admiration and affection for her fellow travellers, saddened by the difficulties some have endured and impressed by their resilience. There is a good mix of people who live different lives in Ireland: the music teacher, the bed-and-breakfast owner, the ceramic artist, the surgeon, the singer, the postman, the psychotherapist, the journalist, the nurse, to name just a few. The one thing they have in common is a wonderful *joie de vivre* and concern for those who need a helping hand. They greet each day with enthusiasm and energy and have chosen to come to Malawi to see at first hand the work of the Sunergy Project.

It's run by a Tipperary couple, Seamus and Elizabeth Hayes. I first got to know Seamus in 2002 when he asked me to lead the Self Help trek to Eritrea. He was assistant director with the organisation, a former president of Macra na Feirme, a good man for the job with a background in dairy farming. Under his leadership, I have travelled to Ethiopia, Malawi and Tanzania with Self Help and, later, Playing for Life. Seamus is now retired but his commitment to the developing world is ongoing. He stayed in touch with Winston Chiawa, former country director in Malawi with Self Help, and Sunergy was formed.

When Winston retired, he opted to forgo a pension in favour of a lump sum with which he bought a plot of land in Nangoma where he was born. It's a village with a population of about five hundred families; the livelihood of the people depends on farming. Irrigation is, of course, a challenge, although they must have been clapping their hands with glee the night we arrived in Blantyre.

Winston donated the plot to his community, and he and Seamus, with a small group of supportive friends in Ireland, set about installing a solar-powered water pump, with pipes that transport water from Lake Malawi to the various farms in the village. It emerges via a tap in the centre of a field to which the farmer can attach his hose and water his crops during the dry season, which stretches from April to November. It's a simple system and it works.

This year's crop yields will be the second since Sunergy was founded. There are sixty-one families in the cooperative thus far, and the idea is to stretch the piping and taps to more farms with continued funding.

The Nangoma sewing group.

Meanwhile, Seamus's wife, Elizabeth, a retired home-economics teacher, has started a sewing group with the women of Nangoma. They have three sewing machines so far, thanks largely to money raised by the Waterford women who skinny-dip to fundraise for the group. Elizabeth has charts and diagrams she attaches to the window of a car, her blackboard, and her sewing classes take place under the shade of a huge leafy tree.

The good news is that the foundations have been built for a small centre that will house the sewing group. It was an absolute joy to arrive in the village and be greeted by the women, who sang and danced to welcome us, and later proudly showed us the cloth bags they had sewn together that morning. Next they would be making a blouse, using paper patterns Elizabeth had brought from Ireland. The women are hard-working and eager to learn to sew, which will not only help them make clothes for their families but, in the future, provide a source of income in this impoverished part of Africa.

We visited some of the houses in Nangoma, shown around by the women who were delighted to welcome us into their homes. Families of up to six are living in dark single-storey houses, some with mud walls, the more secure with rough local brick. They have thatched roofs and clay floors. All are dark inside because there is no electricity. A curtain hanging on a wire separates the sleeping quarters from the main room, which is a tiny

area, with basins, pots and other cooking utensils stacked in a corner. Clothes are stored in plastic bags and hang from a wire under the ceiling. There is no furniture. The family cooks and eats outdoors. When asked what they would like for their homes, some said a floor, others wanted a table or chairs. Not much to ask, really, but unattainable under their present circumstances.

We all know the excitement we feel when we get a new carpet or paint a room. Can you imagine what it would be like for the women in Nangoma to look forward to a few additions to their homes? They deserve the best but they make do with nothing. Hopefully, as the sewing group gains momentum and their skills become established, they will be able to treat themselves and their families to some of the things they would dearly love to have and that we in our homes take for granted.

It was a privilege to be welcomed into the homes of such resilient, fun-loving women who sing and dance their way through their working day.

They have joy in their hearts and a wonderful sense of community. It was also a pleasure to walk the land, escorted by the farmers in the group and see their crops flourishing, thanks to the Sunergy irrigation system. Wasn't it a happy day when Seamus Hayes and Winston Chiawa met back in 1996? Two men from different continents, united initially by the fact that they both worked for the same organisation but both instilled with the desire to help others less fortunate than themselves. Their friendship has endured for more than two decades, as has their desire to improve the lives of the people of Nangoma.

Sunergy is a tiny project. It's not going to change the world but it's certainly changing the lives of this small community. I'm reminded of the words of Mother Teresa: 'Don't think about the numbers. Just help one person at a time.'

Or thirty people at a time, as is the case with Gena Heraty, a Mayo woman who has been living in Haiti for twenty-five years, caring for children and adults with physical and intellectual disabilities. Nos Petits Frères et Soeurs (Our Little Brothers and Sisters) Orphanage

is high up in the mountains in Kenscoff, about fifteen kilometres from Port-au-Prince. It is home to about two hundred Haitian orphans, and Gena looks after the thirty with special needs.

They vary in age from seven to the eldest, Yvonne, a woman of forty, who is full of love and insists on hugging everybody she meets. There is always a smile on her face and also on the faces of Gena's charges, even though some struggle to control their movements and facial expressions.

'Sometimes I feel so powerless
  when I see how much some struggle.
  Just to make it through each day
  can be quite a juggle.
  But what is most amazing
  is the smile that comes so fast.
  No matter how hard they battle,
  these smiles are here to last.'

I can vouch for the truth of what Gena says in her poem about 'her children', and her love for them is plain to see. Gena has a house on the orphanage campus where she lives with all of the children, and where their every need is met with care, compassion and love. They are her priority and her own needs come way down the list. She has provided a loving home for those who were abandoned at birth or in their early years by families who were either too poor to countenance raising them or just didn't want to keep a baby with special needs.

Gena regularly takes calls from the hospital in Pétion-Ville informing her of another abandoned baby. She speaks proudly of her children and how they have thrived with care and love: the boy who wasn't supposed to live past three and is now fourteen, the children who were confined to wheelchairs and now walk, run or limp to greet her when she returns from a trip to the city, happy to have their loving mother at home.

When I visited Gena's home I was struck by the way in which everything is geared towards the care of these vulnerable people, who are thriving and blossoming because they have a loving mother figure and a secure, loving home. The house is bustling with activity, as you would expect with thirty plus people living there. The kitchen is very large and there are high chairs and wheelchairs, toys and therapy equipment throughout the house. From the moment I crossed the threshold I sensed this was a warm, happy place where people were living, in Gena's words, 'their best life'.

Here was another type of home, different from those I had visited in Malawi earlier in the year – and very different from home as we understand it and in which Gena grew up in the townland of Liscarney, outside picturesque Westport. Gena is the second youngest of

Having the craic, with the women of Nangoma.

eleven children. Her father died in 2014 and her mother still lives in the family home, surrounded by a loving, outgoing family of children and grandchildren. It's a happy home that Gena left behind in Mayo, but as TS Eliot wrote: 'Home is where one starts from.'

That Gena Heraty started from a loving, welcoming, bustling home has served her well in Haiti, where she has opened her heart and devoted her life to the most vulnerable, unwanted members of society. You couldn't ask for a better example of home than Gena's or a better illustration of her calling than she gives us in her poem:

> 'These smiles fill me up
> and their love makes me strong,
> they inspire me each day,
> each life a love song.'

We can be proud of people like Gena who, having grown up in the comfort of an Irish home, have reached out to alleviate the struggles that some people must face in their daily lives. I met other caring Irish individuals and groups when I travelled to Haiti, a once beautiful island in the Caribbean that was ravaged by the earthquake of 2010. It killed more than 200,000 people, injured up to 300,000 and left more than a million homeless.

More recently, in 2016, Hurricane Matthew killed nine hundred people and caused almost two billion dollars' worth of damage. I cannot imagine how I would feel if my house was destroyed, the home I have built up and filled with memories and objects of sentimental value. And that's before I begin to register that I would have no shelter, no roof over my head. Such has been the reality for so many Haitian people over several years, and the Irish have a high profile in the restoration projects in the country.

Sister Rose Kelly, another Mayo woman, from Castlebar, lives and works in Jean Rabel in the north-west of the country, where she has built houses for families who were living under corrugated-iron lean-to structures. She has built and runs several schools as well as women's craft groups. She provides a beacon of light for the people in this remote part of Haiti, who felt devastated, abandoned and perhaps forgotten in the aftermath of the earthquake, when the focus was mainly on the capital, Port-au-Prince.

Sister Rose is a bundle of energy and fun, and is known to travel around her communities on a quad bike. She has a highly defined can-do attitude, as does Sister Helen Ryder, from Banagher in County Offaly, who teaches in Port-au-Prince and volunteers in a young offenders' prison, where children as young as nine are held, some for crimes such as stealing food to eat.

Concern, Haven and the Digicel Foundation are all visible in Haiti, reaching out to the stricken people and helping them rebuild their lives. Concern's work revolves around agricultural projects on the offshore island of Île-à-Vache, and a peace-and-reconciliation project among the gangs of the capital city. Haven's projects are concerned with building houses, and the Digicel Foundation has rebuilt 175 schools, destroyed by the earthquake. Irish people are making a significant contribution to the restoration of house and home for people who have suffered and lost so much. I believe they are inspired by a sense of caring and social justice that is deeply connected to our experience of family, home and community.

The Irish people in Haiti exemplify the philosophy of APJ Abdul Kalam, the eleventh President of India, who died in 2015.

> ‘Where there is righteousness in the heart, there is beauty in the character. When there is beauty in the character, there is harmony in the home. When there is harmony in the home, there is order in the nation. When there is order in the nation, there is peace in the world.’

Kalam's words speak of righteousness, beauty, character, harmony, order and peace, qualities that he espoused in his own life. He was the youngest of five, very close to his sister and brothers, and while he remained a lifelong bachelor, he made a habit of sending money to his siblings and their families.

Kalam led a simple life, owned few material possessions and was a devout Muslim, who practised great respect for all religions. He suffered a stroke and died while delivering a lecture at the age of eighty-three and was buried in his hometown of Rameshwaram. Home and family were important to him throughout his life. He was greatly mourned and buried with full state honours: a man who reached out to others from his own understanding of what is right and good, a man of honour and compassion.

Gena Heraty and the other Irish I've mentioned know what it's like to have a happy, secure home. They understand that this is a privilege they have enjoyed. Their compassion, their empathy, their awareness of the inequity of the world and their determination to make a difference extends from that understanding. What the Roman philosopher Pliny the Elder said more than two thousand years ago is as true today as it was then: 'Home is where the heart is.'

Wedding Bells

'Consent your heart to greet the stars coming out a little earlier in the evening.

So when the sun gives in and the night is king – you can take comfort in the company you're sitting in.

Light yourselves candles and be safe in knowing that there is a place for your heart where it will be well protected by the other you've chosen.'

Those words will always be linked with one of the most joyful times of my life: the marriage of my elder daughter, Eva, in November 2016. They are the opening lines of the Reflection after Communion, written and spoken by her brother Tom. Eva and Benny, her fiancé then, her husband now, invited Tom to write the Reflection because he has a lovely way with words and produces a blog from time to time. They were delighted with his composition, and doubly so when, a couple of months after the wedding, he had it printed on vellum and framed, then gave it to Eva as a birthday present.

I love the warmth and security of home that Tom shows us from the very first lines, and I'm glad that my sense of home as a sanctuary seems to have passed to the next generation. That Reflection is a treasured reminder of a wonderfully happy day, the culmination of months of preparation, personal involvement and hard work.

Eva and Benny got engaged in New York during their holiday in the States in August 2015. I was putting the finishing touches to my last book, *What Matters*, when the news came through so I dedicated it to them, wishing them lots of happiness.

The celebrations began as soon as they returned from the US and made their way to Tralee, where the family was gathered for the Rose of Tralee Festival. I was chairing the judging panel and the festival committee, and my fellow judges made their way to my room for a party, with Prosecco, strawberries, hugs and kisses. Eva and Benny left Tralee the next day and I returned to my judging duties.

As soon as I got back to Dublin I went into planning mode for the official engagement party, which, naturally enough, would happen in my house. I had a reputation to keep up, after all. Every event must be celebrated and the first engagement in either our family or Benny's was right up there in terms of celebratory entitlement.

A week of preparation ensued, covering all the bases of cooking, gardening, cleaning windows and, yes, you're right, putting up a few decorations! The theme was white, obviously, and the house was festooned with paper doves and wedding bells, and white rose-covered fairy lights, battery-operated so they could be positioned in every nook and cranny of the house and garden. The tablecloths were white damask, strewn with silver and white confetti. The porch was decorated with white candles and lanterns, there was a wreath of white roses on the hall door and, believe it or not, the sun shone. It was a balmy evening at the end of August and everyone ate in the back garden, laughed and sang into the wee small hours. A happy and fun end to summer gatherings, and a fitting start to the anticipation of Eva and Benny's wedding. They booked the church and the hotel, then settled back into work.

Christmas had an extra special feel to it that year, and as soon as January arrived, it was time to think about wedding dresses, and if choosing a wedding dress is not a cause for celebration, then I don't know what is. On a bright, brisk Saturday morning, Eva, my friend Anita, Lucy, who had returned from Australia shortly after the engagement was announced, and I headed off to visit four bridal shops in Kilkenny. We decided to make a weekend of it so we booked into a hotel in the city and had a lovely time dress-shopping and touring, having dinner and talking. No decision was made that weekend, but a shortlist was drawn up.

Eventually Eva settled on a beautiful beaded gown and veil by Don O'Neill, the Kerry-born, New York-based designer, renowned for dressing people like Oprah Winfrey and other Hollywood stars. Saying 'yes to the dress' necessitated another visit to Kilkenny a few months later. The same foursome headed to the 'Marble City'. We didn't stay over this time but we did mark the occasion by having afternoon tea in Langton's Wedgewood Rooms, a gentle celebration of this important moment in Eva's life, with lots of tea and cakes and some lovely vegan options for Lucy.

There were many meaningful aspects to Eva and Benny's wedding, and the choice of dress and veil was certainly one of them. Every bride looks beautiful on her wedding day and Eva was magnificent, in my unbiased motherly opinion! Don O'Neill who created the Theia gown Eva chose is a good friend. In fact Eva and Benny had dinner with him and his fiancé Pascal in New York the evening after Benny proposed the previous summer.

What a lovely occasion it must have been, two engaged couples exchanging stories and making plans. Don and Pascal have been together twenty-five years now and got engaged following the marriage equality referendum in May 2015. I couldn't imagine better company for Eva and Benny to share their excitement with.

Don and Pascal got married in June 2016 and invited Eva and me to their wedding. It was a most joyous celebration in Don's home village of Ballyheigue in County Kerry. He designed the stylish grey wedding suits for himself and Pascal. They were embroidered with a fuchsia motif, Don's late mother Mim's favourite flower. The fuchsia theme continued in the flower arrangements on the dinner tables, and when Don and Pascal removed their jackets for the dancing, they were wearing crisp white shirts with the same fuchsia motif.

The happiness and fun of that wedding began with Don and Pascal walking up the hill to the golf club in Ballyheigue. They were smiling broadly, holding hands and carrying a helium-filled heart-shaped balloon each, which they released into the air as they arrived to loud cheers from the assembled guests, family and friends. We were all swept along on the tide of love, goodwill

Myself and Eva with Don (inside right) and his husband Pascal.

and sheer joy. Eva and I were honoured to be there and the celebrations continued the following day, with a lunch party for Don's fiftieth birthday.

Theirs was a great wedding, made all the more special because they'd had to wait so long before it was legally possible for them, two gay men, to exchange their vows of love for each other. I am proud that the Irish people voted so overwhelmingly in favour of equality for all in the May 2015 referendum. Don and Pascal's weekend was imbued, from start to finish, with love and support for the happy couple.

I consider it a stroke of serendipity that Eva chose a wedding dress designed by her friend. And what a dress! It was a work of art, elegant, timeless, beaded from top to toe, with a beautiful scooped neckline and back, and pretty cap sleeves trimmed with teardrop beads. The veil was magnificent also. In fact Eva fell in love with the veil before she'd chosen a dress. Whatever dress she settled on had to suit that veil! It was long, cathedral length, I believe they call it, dotted with little petals of white tulle and trailed beautifully behind Eva as she walked up the aisle. As soon as she laid eyes on it she knew she had to have it. I don't know of any other bride who chose the veil before she had decided on the dress.

But I'm jumping ahead! Dress and veil sorted, there was still a lot to be organised before that special date of 5 November 2016. I have great admiration for Eva and Benny. They did all of the work themselves, and the personal touches were clear, and special. Their kitchen table and sometimes the dining room morphed into a workstation. There were bags everywhere filled with paper, candles, glue, ribbon, glitter, whatever was needed for the preparations. I have to admit there were times when I would have liked to remove the lot and get some order back into the house but, in hindsight, I'm delighted that the run-up to this wedding was a central part of our family life and glad that Eva and Benny could lay out all their stuff in the comfort of Eva's home. Wouldn't it have been very short-sighted of me to make a fuss about clutter? It was a privilege to be involved in every aspect of the preparation.

Eva and Benny bought three different sizes of paper and made the invitations by laying the sheets on top of each other and attaching them with gold ribbon. Each invitation was placed in an envelope and sealed with a circular sticker, their initials printed on it. They ordered them online, white, and the colour had to be changed to bronze: they rubbed the stickers with a damp teabag and allowed them to dry before attaching them to the envelopes.

They also ordered wooden letters online, a capital E and B, about three hundred of them, and painted them bronze, with the help of friends, ready to be placed on every table at the reception. You're getting the message by now, I'd say, that the colour scheme for the wedding was bronze, nice and warm for the time of year and reflective of the bridesmaids' sequined bronze dresses. Lucy and Eva's cousin Clare were the bridesmaids, and they took their duties seriously, organising the hen party, then keeping that voluminous veil extended so that we could all see the petals in the church on the wedding day!

I'm really proud that Eva made and iced the wedding cake, four tiers, two fruit and two biscuit. She took lessons in sugarcraft and made all the decorative roses and leaves. Now, that was a finicky job! Each petal had to be made separately, then shaped and joined with

others to form a rose, painted and dusted with gold colouring. The leaves had to be shaped, painted and the veins coloured a darker green. A slow, painstaking task. Not for the faint-hearted. And not helped after a leaf-making session by Daisy, our cheeky and constantly hungry dog: she jumped on to the table and helped herself to the drying sugarcraft.

The cake was assembled in the kitchen, placed on a big platter and transported with much trepidation to the hotel the day before the wedding in the back of the best man's car. Helen, his wife, cradled it like a baby and roared at her husband to drive slowly over the bumps. No pressure! I'd say Ray, Benny's friend and best man, would like to have renegotiated the terms and conditions of his role. He was petrified the cake would fall apart before he got it to its destination. Who said a best man had simply to look after the groom and keep him calm? Poor Ray's nerves were in tatters when he arrived back from the hotel.

Eva and Benny's wedding reception was held in the Morrison Hotel on Ormond Quay, a lovely Dublin city venue close to the Ha'penny Bridge. Its location gave the bride another idea for some more make and do. She and Benny decided to name the tables after bridges on the Liffey. Did you know that there are twenty-three bridges over the river? There were sixteen tables at the wedding and each was called after one of the city bridges. Eva and Benny got a tourist map of Dublin, enlarged the section that showed the Liffey and attached it to a big board. They positioned the table plan around the map and, with strips of gold ribbon, made lines from the table list to the bridges after which they were named. Another session at the kitchen table, another time-consuming, but very personal touch, which the guests appreciated.

The run-up to the wedding wasn't all about making invitations, cakes and table plans, though. There was a lot of fun and frolics during the spring and summer also. The house was transformed into a beauty salon one fine Saturday evening in May when we had a hair and make-up night, a kind of alternative hen party. Our two local hairdressers and make-up artist came along and set up stations around the house where the guests, all women, could get a fancy hairdo and their make-up done. The decorations and lights that had been put away after the engagement party got a second airing. We had supper and Prosecco, and Eva made and iced a chocolate biscuit cake, a kind of wedding preview and a practice run for her. It was a happy, laughter-filled night, the essence of home for me, and once again we were lucky with the weather. We sat outdoors, and I'm sure I don't need to tell you what the conversation revolved around!

Over the summer we had a few more afternoon-tea outings. In fact, Lucy and cousin Clare included an

Alice in Wonderland-themed afternoon tea as one of the activities for Eva's hen party. They rented bungalows in the grounds of Waterford Castle and after tea they adjourned to a roller disco before heading out to dinner. They had a great weekend by all accounts. I didn't go to the hen party. Leave them at it, I say. It's for their generation, I believe.

We had no shortage of other wedding-themed celebrations. I spent the summer gathering little gifts, which I wrapped and presented to Eva and Benny as a surprise the weekend before the wedding. Simple things, like tea towels with hearts on them, a photo frame, their initials in colourful pottery, heart-shaped measuring cups. You'd be surprised at the amount of items in shops that are heart-shaped. I could have filled a trunk with them! The happy couple got a kick out of unwrapping each little thing, a bit like opening stockings on Christmas morning.

Apart from the heart-shaped gift fest, that weekend provided a hiatus from the W-word because Saturday, 29 October, was Tom's thirtieth birthday. You're probably thinking that with all the W preparations, it would make sense to celebrate the birthday in a restaurant, perhaps, and let somebody else do the cooking. Tom, in fairness to him, suggested that this would be the thing to do.

Heck, no! We'd had a big house party for Eva's

thirtieth a few years ago and, anyway, the attic is full of tasteful-ish Halloween decorations. For one night only, the pretty white wedding-themed candles and decorations were left to one side and the colour scheme was orange and black. There were witches, spiders, ghosts and ghouls scattered around the place and we had a wonderful evening. Eva took time out of a pretty hectic W schedule to make a pumpkin chocolate cake, decorated in good old orange and black, very different from the sugarcraft roses and leaves she'd been working on all summer.

A highlight for me just before the Big Day was an overnight in a hotel with my two daughters. I had been debating with myself whether we could spare the time a few days before the wedding. So many things have to be accomplished in that final week, not least returning all the Halloween paraphernalia to the attic and recreating the wedding wonderland in the house. There were lots of trips hither and thither, a lot of picking up and delivering.

There was indeed a bit of a dash at the end, but I'm so glad we had that night away. It was a quiet, relaxed time out, an opportunity to draw breath and relish the moment, to allow the sense to sink in of the occasion to which we were so looking forward. There was a stillness about that night, which I savoured. As the sixth-century Chinese philosopher Lao Tzu wrote: 'Be still. Stillness reveals the secrets of eternity.'

126

We decluttered our minds: there was no talk of jobs that needed to be done. This was a moment to reflect on what it would feel like to be the bride, the bridesmaid, the mother of the bride. This was the first time for each of us to live our roles and imagine how we would feel when all the preparation and build-up drew to a natural conclusion four days later.

To say that the reality was even better than the anticipation is an understatement. We were all swept along on a sea of joy from the moment we opened our eyes on the morning of the wedding. Don't worry. There's a minute-by-minute diary of the day coming up before this chapter ends.

Some of my friends thought I had contracted wedding fever, such was the number of gatherings I threw that year but I'm glad I organised every single one. It's a very happy time in the life of a young couple, of a son or daughter, brother or sister. The whole family is in celebratory and supportive mode, and that in itself is worthy of a happy gathering.

I'm also glad that Eva was married from home, the place where she grew up, where she is comfortable, relaxed, surrounded by her own things. For me, home is a sanctuary, a place of comfort and security. I'd hope that my children feel the same way. The American writer Gladys M. Hunt defined home very nicely in *Honey for a Child's Heart*:

‘It's a place where people share and understand each other. Its relationships are nurturing. The people in it do not have to be perfect; instead, they need to be honest, loving, supportive, recognising a common humanity that makes all of us vulnerable.’

My home was Wedding HQ prior to Eva and Benny's wedding. It's as well there's a spare room and a big shed because every spare inch was taken up with wedding paraphernalia for months beforehand. The night before the wedding was a quiet time in the house. Both bridesmaids stayed with the bride, of course, and we were also joined by my sister Deirdre, Eva's godmother. I have lovely memories of that evening. Eva bought beautiful Chupi jewellery for Lucy and Clare, and matching pyjamas for us all, a photo op naturally on the landing before we headed to bed.

When the house was quiet, Eva lay beside me on my bed for a while and I held her hand and reflected on the time that had flown by since she was a baby, my first-born and the first grandchild on both sides of her family. I remembered vividly the excitement and joy that greeted her birth. I couldn't have known the excitement and joy that awaited us in a few short hours when the darkness gave way to the morning light on her wedding day.

We all slept well and awoke to a bright blue cloudless sky, not bad for 5 November. A clear advantage to a winter wedding is that there is no talk about what the weather will be like on the day. When people get married in the summer in Ireland, it's an issue. Everyone wants the sun to shine. The weather app on the phone is constantly checked. There's talk about the long- and medium-range forecast. The Child of Prague statue is placed under a bush, more in hope than expectation, and if it rains, as it often does, let's face it, there is understandable disappointment. If you're getting married in the winter, you have no right to be disappointed if the weather is bad. Everyone knew it was going to be cold, but to wake up to a blue sky was a huge bonus. We couldn't believe our luck.

The early morning was a special time and I have memories that I will cherish always. We arrived in the kitchen in our matching PJs, and at half past seven, on the button, my friend Anita and her husband Michael rang the doorbell. They were laden with food, which they placed on the kitchen table, then left. I'd say their visit lasted about five minutes. When we uncovered the dishes, we discovered an absolute feast. They had cooked breakfast for us. There was a colourful fruit salad in a crystal bowl, and on separate plates, smoked salmon, bacon, scrambled eggs, grilled mushrooms, tomatoes, plus vegan sausages and special potato cakes

that their son, John, had made for Lucy. That breakfast was delicious and we ate it with gusto, marvelling at this act of kindness and friendship, which got the day off to a fabulous start.

At eight o'clock, on the button (a lot of things happened on the button that day), the doorbell rang again and Gillian and Louise, the two hairdressers, and Rachel, the make-up artist, arrived with the tools of their trade. You'll remember them, of course, from our hair and make-up night. They set up their stations in the kitchen and went to work. The table that had been heaving under a feast minutes beforehand was now heaving under hairdryers, tongs, pins, make-up and mirrors. Let battle commence!

There were lots of laughs, lots of chat, lots of photos taken, and all in a calm, happy environment. I loved the simple nature of Eva's wedding morning, and enjoyed all of the different elements as they fell into place, the doorbell ringing again and again. On the button! And I was honoured that all of the excitement was happening in the kitchen at the heart of the home.

Hats off to Eva and Benny. Their preparation had involved working backwards from one o'clock, the time of the mass. Not exactly on the button this time, but that's allowed. They'd left plenty of time for everything so there was no rush and certainly no fuss. There was a lot of emotion, though. I thought my heart would burst when I walked into Eva's bedroom and saw Lucy and Clare in their beautiful bronze dresses, fixing Eva's gown

Deirdre, Eva's godmother, before leaving for the church to practice her surprise song.

and attaching her beloved petal veil to the headpiece on which she had attached a gold pin that had belonged to Benny's granny. This was a surprise for Benny. He and his mother were so touched that the pin was part of the ensemble.

Eva was radiant and calm, a beautiful bride, and I ached to throw my arms around her and give her a big hug. I didn't, though, in case she cried and smudged her make-up. I just stood and gazed at her, and wiped a tear from my own eye. We smiled at each other, a beautiful moment, filled with love, that I carry in my heart to this day. Then it was downstairs and into the kitchen where the family had gathered to wish Eva well and to see the dress. It had remained a secret, despite lots of speculation as to style, make, fabric and finish.

In fact, there was so much talk about the dress beforehand, I'm surprised Tom and Eoin's girlfriends didn't open a book on what it would look like. Just as well they didn't, though, because they would have lost

A beautiful bride, and two beautiful bridesmaids, Lucy (left) and Clare – not feeling the cold!

their shirts on the bet. They were way off the mark in their speculation, and both just said, 'Wow!' when Eva walked into the kitchen. As did the neighbours who had come to the house to see her off. I was delighted to have them there. Another nice aspect of getting married from home. Those people who had seen Eva grow up were there to wish her well as she embarked on married life. The goodwill of the people in the kitchen and of the others who came out onto the road to see Eva as she left the house was almost palpable, and full of warmth.

That special yet simple morning came to its natural conclusion with everybody emerging from our home, suited, booted and heading for the church, the next part of what was turning out to be a really lovely day. And I'm not just talking about the blue November sky!

My brother Tony was the official bridal chauffeur. He had polished his car and put a ribbon on the bonnet and it looked a million dollars. It saved Eva and Benny a bit less than a million dollars but a car was one expense they hadn't had to think about. The personal touches that Tony included added to the loveliness of the day. There was bottled water for Eva, her dad and me, as we drove the two kilometres to the Church of the Annunciation in Rathfarnham, and following the ceremony, when Tony was driving the newlyweds from the church to the hotel, glasses of Prosecco and, in a pottery bowl, strawberries skewered on cocktail sticks to avoid juice getting on hands and perhaps on the white dress. Aaagh! Perish that thought.

The sight that greeted us when Tony drove into the churchyard was unexpected and wonderful. Don, who had designed Eva's wedding gown, and Pascal, his husband, were standing in the porch, all smiles, waiting for Eva to arrive so that Don could fix her veil and make sure that everything was just so with the dress before she walked up the aisle. What a thoughtful thing to do. This was a day off for them. They had flown in from New York as wedding guests. As soon as they'd received their invitation in the post, they'd emailed to say they had immediately booked their flights. And here they were, in their light wedding suits, waiting on the church step, on a November day that was radiant in its blue sky but icy cold, to lend a hand. Another instance of kindness on a day that seemed to be punctuated by acts of love and thoughtfulness from beginning to end.

Eva was escorted up the aisle by her father and mother, and the sight of friends and family gathered in the pews, smiling and taking photos, was uplifting and magical. I held her hand as we floated up that aisle. I was delighted to be escorting her to her future husband, a kind, good man, whose heart I would say was pounding as he listened to the music and waited.

In fact, the video shows that the colour had totally drained out of Benny's face. His lips were white and he

Here comes the bride – accompanied by her Mam and Dad.

just stared ahead, anticipating, I suppose, the moment when he would behold his bride. That moment arrived and, as he turned to her, the colour returned to his cheeks and all was well.

Eva and Benny had put a lot of work into the marriage mass and it was a very special part of the day. When was the last time you heard anyone say they would have liked a church service to go on longer? Well, it happened that day. Everyone loved the mass. Father Liam Lawton, a dear friend for many years, was the celebrant and the mass reflected his gentle, unpretentious and unassuming personality. There was reverence, chat and a smile along the way, and when he pronounced Eva and Benny husband and wife, Benny turned towards the guests and punched the air to rapturous applause.

The music was an integral part of the service. The Palestrina Choir, friends of mine for a number of years, had offered to sing, and between the boys and gentlemen of the choir, their organ scholar Robbie Carroll and my sister Deirdre, the music from beginning to end was heavenly.

Eva walked up the aisle to Robbie playing 'The Arrival of the Queen of Sheba', followed immediately by Psalm 103, the uplifting 'Praise My Soul'. Eva and Benny walked down the aisle as husband and wife to the strains of Handel's 'Hallelujah Chorus' and in between there were many musical gems: Mozart's 'Sanctus, Agnus Dei' and 'Ave Verum'; two of Liam Lawton's compositions, 'The Cloud's Veil' and 'Allelú'; and some beautiful traditional pieces, like 'A Mhuire Mháthair' and 'Dúlamán'.

The musical highlight of the wedding ceremony was undoubtedly Deirdre's special song in honour of Eva and Benny. Let me take you back to when Eva was a young child, first granddaughter and Deirdre's goddaughter. A lot of firsts and here's another. Her first trip to the movies was to see *Beauty and the Beast*. Who brought her? Auntie Deirdre. What's her favourite movie of all time? *Beauty and the Beast*. What T-shirt did she buy last Thursday in Penneys? A *Beauty and the Beast* T-shirt.

2017 saw the release of a new version of the movie Eva had fallen in love with back in 1991, when she and Deirdre headed off to the recently opened Square in Tallaght. The opening was a big occasion. Forty-five thousand people turned up to celebrate what was then the largest shopping centre in Ireland. Charlie Haughey, as Taoiseach, did the honours. Gay Byrne hosted his radio show from the Crow's Nest there to mark the occasion. If he had known that a little seven-year-old girl from Knocklyon would walk out of the cinema complex soon afterwards enraptured by *Beauty and the Beast*, and that twenty-five years later her godmother would personalise 'Tale as Old as Time' for her niece's wedding ceremony I think he would have been pleased.

I hope in his stag quiz Benny was asked Eva's favourite movie. He would have scored ten! Eva has form, I have to say. *Beauty and the Beast* is her favourite movie and *Murder She Wrote* is her favourite TV show. The fact that Angela Lansbury stars in both provides a certain continuity and serendipity. Jessica Fletcher, the sleuth Ms Lansbury played, was a regular in our TV room on rainy afternoons when Eva was in secondary school. I don't know if she realised then that, as Mrs Tea Pot, Ms Lansbury sang the song that has been a constant in Eva's life since she saw the movie in the Square, through the years of watching the movie on video, to the beautiful moment when her aunt-godmother sang it for her and her new husband on their wedding day. Now as a married woman she's walking around East Limerick in a *Beauty and the Beast* T-shirt!

Back to November 2016 and the Church of the Annunciation in Rathfarnham. Eva was delighted and flabbergasted when Deirdre's adaptation of 'Tale as Old as Time' began, then in came a haunting interlude on a saxophone. Deirdre had asked a friend to play during the song. 'Momentous' does not describe the momentousness of the moment. Deirdre told me afterwards that they had practised during the week in a friend's kitchen and felt this was something special. They were right. It was.

Eva and Benny stood at the altar while Deirdre, with her friend Tony on the saxophone, epitomised the sense of what the marriage ceremony was all about. Beautiful moments captured simply and warmly without fanfare or palaver. This was Eva and Benny's day and certain elements made it special for them and everyone else.

I spoke earlier about one of the advantages of a winter wedding being that there is no talk beforehand about the weather. There is another to be recorded here. Although it was a bright sunny day, it was cold, so the greetings and photographs in the churchyard were … efficiently managed, shall we say? There was no hanging about: the light was fading and there were photos to be taken of the bride and groom at the Ha'penny Bridge. Guests made their way to The Morrison Hotel. During the drinks reception, there was a PowerPoint presentation of family photos: in the weeks before the wedding, Eva and Benny had gathered all the photos from both families and put them on a USB stick.

It was well worth it, I think – but then I would, given my penchant for my digital photo frame in the kitchen, a lovely way of reliving happy moments. Guests were entertained by a magician while they waited for Eva and Benny, who were smiling and shivering on the bridge across the road. The magician was Benny's idea, an inspired one. He established a tone of magic, surprise, laughter and unbridled joy, which persisted right through the evening.

As I've said, each table was named after a bridge on the Liffey, and Rory Wolahan, a close family friend and my godson, had executed a line drawing of each bridge and framed them, to decorate the tables. In every aspect of the reception there was a sense of connection to family and to Dublin city, which was wholesome and seemed to make so much sense. You don't need me to tell you that we're capable of needlessly losing the run of ourselves when it comes to weddings, and I believe that when we look back on a family wedding that connection is precious. It was further illustrated by Eva and Benny's first dance.

They had asked singer-songwriter Dermot, my brother John's son, to sing and play the guitar as they took to the floor, and had spent a lot of time choosing the song.

I remember we were all gathered in the conservatory one summer's evening when they announced that they had settled on Christina Perri's beautiful 'A Thousand Years'. Clare brought the words up on the cracked

The first dance.

screen of her phone and held them aloft for Dermot to sing. It was such an emotional moment. I cried, Eva cried and Eileen, Dermot's mother, cried. And we were just sitting in the conservatory listening to Dermot trying to make out the words on Clare's cracked phone screen! Add to the mix that Eva and Benny had had dancing lessons, and I'm sure you won't be surprised to hear that the tears flowed in The Morrison when the bride and groom took to the floor. Dermot sang, and they danced, surrounded by the people who loved them best. It wasn't just the mammies who were teary either. A beautiful moment, filled with love and happiness.

I'd recommend anyone to listen to that song that speaks of time bringing two hearts together and the feeling that they have loved each other for a thousand years and that their love will continue for a thousand more. It will do your heart good.

A happy day, the culmination of months of preparation, but what to do on the next? Why not have a house party on Sunday? Mad or what? This necessitated precise forward planning, given that we stayed in the hotel on the night of the wedding.

To say that the party was organised with military precision doesn't do it justice. A one-pot wonder had to be on the menu so Anita and I made industrial quantities of Hungarian goulash two days before the Big Day and a vegetable chilli for vegetarians and vegans. The rice was cooked and ready to be heated in the oven. There'd be wedding cake for dessert. Fires were set. Candles ready to be lit. Champagne chilling in the fridge.

When I arrived home at lunchtime on Sunday, an army of volunteers had the house looking absolutely magnificent. It was a wonderland of fairy lights, candles, wedding decorations, and the inviting scent of goulash and chilli wafting from the kitchen. All that was missing were the guests. Not for long, though.

By about six o'clock every room in the house was jammed. At one point I wanted to get a bowl from the dresser at the opposite side of the kitchen but couldn't make a path there. So it was back to the sink and a quick wash-up. We had a fabulous jamboree, singing, laughing, chatting into the wee small hours. Despite my worry that we were taking on a bit much, everything went swimmingly, and even if it hadn't, nobody would have cared. This was an opportunity to continue the celebration in an informal and fun way, and being at home just added to the magic.

Eva and Benny's wedding was the first in my family. I loved every minute of it and for me it was a reminder that family and friends are what make life meaningful. There was an outpouring of nurturing love and support at every juncture. The nuptials involved a lot of hard work so I was glad I had held onto my holidays and taken two full weeks off beforehand.

After the wedding, when the clear-up was finished and the last of the paper doves and bells had been taken down, I felt enveloped in a cloak of love and friendship that would sustain me for a long time to come.

And so Eva and Benny embark on their life together as partners, as husband and wife, as soulmates. My wish for them is encapsulated in the closing lines of Tom's Communion Reflection:

> 'I wish the world for you,
> From your two pairs of hands and your
> two beating hearts.'

Burning Out and the Mindful Message

'*If you want to conquer the anxiety of life, live in the moment, live in the breath.*'

Amit Ray

In the middle of the summer last year, I had a eureka moment. It changed my life completely.

It was a Wednesday morning at the end of June. I was in my kitchen, loading the dishwasher after breakfast before heading into the *Nationwide* office at RTÉ in Donnybrook, listening but not really paying attention to Ryan Tubridy on the radio. He was chirping away on the radio when his conversation with a young woman caught my attention. It began to sink in and make more and more sense to me in view of how I was feeling on that day.

The young woman's name was Róisín Agnew and she had written a blog about her decision to leave Ireland and go to live in Lisbon. What's so special about that? Don't we all dream of winning the Lotto, upping sticks and moving to sunnier climes? That's what I was thinking at the start of the interview, but as Róisín continued to talk, I was relating more and more to what she was saying and the reasons for her decision to overhaul her life and move to Portugal.

So how was I feeling on that day? Not good.

> ' I wish I could show you,
>   When you are lonely or in darkness,
>   the astonishing light of your own being.'

I wish the Persian poet Hafiz, who penned those comforting and kind words in the fourteenth century, could have shown me that 'astonishing light' because I had been feeling an acute lack of it for several months. I'm no stranger to life's slings and arrows, the good times and the difficult, challenging periods. I've written about loneliness and feeling down (slightly depressed) in *What Matters*. The response I got, and continue to get, from readers has been overwhelmingly positive and supportive: so many people were pleased to read of my struggles because they resonated with their own. We're all in this together, folks, we do the best we can, and it's a comfort to know that others go through sad, lonely and hard times at different points in their lives. No thinking, feeling, engaging being is immune to the occasional

assault on their sense of wellness, and there are certain stages in life when negativity is more pronounced.

For me, menopause was a low time; my children growing up, having their own adult lives and leaving home was another; and the random days of sadness that come out of left field and creep up unannounced as I get older have been rough but transitory.

This new feeling was different, though. I had never experienced anything like it before. A dull flatness had invaded me and I had been finding it difficult to shift out of its cloudy grey grasp. It tainted my sense of well-being and had taken the lustre off wonderful opportunities and moments since it had crept into my psyche. It had become a very unwelcome guest. I wondered if I was experiencing a sense of anticlimax after the excitement and joy of 2016 and the wedding. For me and my family that was a magical time filled with love and happy moments, lots of hard work in the preparation, lots of fun on the 5th and 6th of November, twelve months of joy, culminating in a glow of satisfaction when the dust settled and Eva and Benny were Mr and Mrs Boland.

After the wedding I'd have loved to spool back and do it all over again. I know Eva and Benny felt the same way. We made the most of every occasion – some would say we milked every occasion! – and I have nothing but happy memories of a great year and a great family-and-friends event in all our lives.

I can't say the same for the following year, though. From the start, 2017 was shaping up to be an *annus horribilis*. It began well with New Year celebrations at Eva and Benny's house, followed shortly afterwards by a relaxing week in Lanzarote with a friend. Filming with *Nationwide* was enjoyable as ever.

There is an unfailing welcome for the programme team wherever we go. I remember a most enjoyable day spent in Castleblayney in Monaghan filming a piece with the beloved, sadly since departed singer Big Tom McBride, and his family. The cameraman and I arrived that morning at the golf club to take some shots and we were welcomed with coffee and hot scones. After that we proceeded to the village of Oram and the McBride home, where Tom and his wife Rose's four children, nine grandchildren, and some friends and neighbours greeted us warmly and gave us tea, sandwiches and cake. It's a struggle to keep the weight off, working on this programme, I can assure you!

We filmed the chat, the reminiscence, the laughter, a few songs, then headed to the local community and GAA hall where there's a plaque to Big Tom. His fellow band members, some of whom had been playing with him for more than fifty years, were there to greet us. More reminiscence, then on to the Íontas Arts Centre in Castleblayney, where Tom's wife and I were presented with flowers by the local people who had come together

Filming for Nationwide, with Rita Gilligan, Global Ambassador for Hard Rock Cafe.

to ensure that this legend of country music was honoured in his lifetime with a statue in his hometown. That was why *Nationwide* was there. We went on to the Glencarn Hotel, to meet more of Tom's fans and friends and to eat a lovely buffet supper, organised by Margo O'Donnell, sister of Daniel and dear friend of Tom and Rose.

That day in Castleblayney left me with a warm glow, and the programme I made with Tom and his wife Rose, both of whom died in 2018, will always have a special place in my heart. It's a privilege to work on a programme that shines a positive light on the goodness, creativity, community spirit and enterprise that exists in Ireland. And that warm glow even shone through the thickness of the flat grey cloud as it began to settle in my heart.

As the months progressed I was less and less happy in myself, a feeling very different from the sporadic loneliness or sadness I've come to accept as part of life's rich tapestry. I accept that life is a mixture of happy and sad times, and we appreciate happiness more because we have known sadness.

This new emotion, though, was not sporadic. It was gaining momentum and becoming quite debilitating. I found it increasingly difficult to motivate myself to tackle simple tasks as the months progressed. The ironing was piling up, yet I couldn't bring myself to open the basket. This from a woman who actually enjoys ironing – I have referred to it in the past as 'time out'. I set up the ironing board beside the kettle in the kitchen and iron away to my heart's content, drinking tea, listening to the radio and watching my digital photo frame bring back memories of times spent with family and friends.

That scenario disappeared last year, and the ironing pile got higher and higher. I also found it hard to make myself keep my clothes in order. They were piling up over the back of a chair in my bedroom or thrown into the wardrobe willy-nilly. This habit was alien to me. I feel ashamed even to admit this messy secret.

The year before I had taken great pleasure in following the edicts of one Marie Kondo, the Japanese lifestyle and cleaning guru, who has transformed the lives of countless millions worldwide. I read one of her books, *The Life-Changing Magic of Tidying up: The Japanese Art of Decluttering and Organising*. The method is called KonMari. It's simple and it works. Decluttering entails throwing all of your clothes on the floor – even the items you've had for years, hoping two things: that they'll come back into fashion and that you'll have lost a stone by then!

You take each piece of clothing in your hand and ask yourself, 'Does this spark joy?' If the answer is no, you get rid of it. I found the process liberating. It gave me a feeling of lightness, not to mention the extra space I gained in wardrobes and drawers. And then the organising. KonMari involves rolling clothes and placing them alongside each other in drawers and on shelves, rather than piling them on top of each other. You end up with more space and you can see and easily reach whatever you need.

Marie Kondo is in her thirties and has published four books on organising and tidying, which have sold millions of copies and been published in more than thirty countries. She was listed as one of *Time* magazine's 100 most influential people at the ripe old age of thirty, having been interested in organising and tidying since she was a child in junior school and preferred to be tidying the classroom than doing PE. I'm not sure I'd have liked one of my children to be tidying shelves instead of playing games but it stood Marie in good stead for her future career.

And I can vouch for the KonMari method of keeping only items that spark joy and rolling clothes neatly in drawers. At least, I *could* vouch for it. The grey cloud that enveloped me last year saw me lack the enthusiasm to keep track of my wardrobe. As a rule, I like to be organised. I knew the good feeling that KonMari gave me, and I also knew that the chair I was using for my clothes was definitely not part of that feel-good factor. I couldn't motivate myself to do anything about it, though. When I wasn't working, I found myself wearing the same few sets of clothes. For the record, I washed

Above, on holiday with Mam and Dad, London, 1970. Below, with family at Sherkin Island, 1973.

them between wears but I wasn't ringing the changes. As the weather improved, I continued to wear dark winter clothes. My heart was not in it.

There were other worrying trends that I was noticing about myself. Anyone who knows me is well aware that I enjoy having people to the house and celebrating whenever the occasion demands and sometimes even if it doesn't. We had two lovely gatherings in the house, one in March to mark the fortieth anniversary of my father's death, a fitting tribute to his memory. It was

157

also a nice way for his grandchildren to get to know something of the grandfather who had died at fifty-nine, seven years before Eva, his eldest grandchild, was born. The anniversary fell on a Saturday and we, his four children, two daughters-in-law, with his ten grandchildren and their partners, gathered at the graveside. We laid a garland of lilies, Deirdre sang, and we recited the glorious mysteries of the Rosary.

Afterwards we came back to my house for supper. I had pinpointed photos of Daddy in the various albums that were passed around. We spoke of our memories of this funny and outgoing man, and later watched old family movies taken with the cine camera back in the sixties and seventies. Precious memories were evoked and more memories made on that special day.

The second gathering happened in May and marked Eva and Benny's half-year anniversary. Like I said, the occasion doesn't always have to demand it! Eva and Benny had been away overnight with friends and arrived back on Saturday, 5 May, six months to the day since they were married. Who could resist having a hooley under the circumstances? Don't answer that! It was a first for the guests who turned up, as directed, nice and early. Not only was it a party but a surprise party, so they had to be *in situ* before the guests of honour arrived.

Again the wedding decorations and fairy lights were called into service, a bit bedraggled admittedly but the sentimental value of hanging them in the same places as they had hung for the engagement and wedding celebrations was huge. We observed a definite theme: Hungarian goulash, as we'd had the day after the wedding, chocolate biscuit cake, iced and decorated the same colour as the wedding cake, and a table centrepiece reminiscent of those at the wedding. I hung Eva's wedding dress and veil in the same spot in the dining room where the photographer had placed them on the morning of the wedding and displayed photos of the day for everyone to see. The wedding video played on a loop all evening and everybody dropped in and out of the TV room to remember the day. The balloons were the *pièce de résistance*: helium-filled with the number six on them! They were intended to celebrate a six-year-old's birthday but that's beside the point. They got the message across. The sun shone and the craic was good.

I am writing in animated terms about those two parties last year as a result of the changes I have made following my eureka moment, but at the time my reaction to them was less enthusiastic. I enjoyed planning them enormously, and was delighted that they happened, but I found myself thinking negative, weary thoughts afterwards, and had absolutely no inclination for further celebrations. I became quite morose about gatherings and events and found myself wondering, What's the point? You prepare, you celebrate and then it's over.

I was projecting beyond happy occasions, even before they'd happened, to when they would be over, and the greyness would return. I had to force myself to do anything other than work but force myself I did. I have always been one to embrace any opportunity that presents itself.

I relish travel and have always had boundless energy. I spent a lovely weekend in Paris a few years ago celebrating Mothers' Day with three friends, and as they made their way home to Dublin, I flew to Mozambique and filmed a programme for *Nationwide*. Not a bother on me. Two weeks after Eva and Benny's wedding I spent three days in Cork recording the RTÉ Christmas carols programme with a lovely line-up of guests, including the RTÉ Concert Orchestra, Brian Kennedy, Celine Byrne, The Priests and Enya. Four days later I was flying to Boston for a programme commemorating the centenary of 1916. Home for three days, then off to London to record our *Nationwide Christmas Special* from Kilburn and Cricklewood. Home for two days and back to London for a prearranged weekend of sightseeing with Lucy. All this alongside the usual filming duties of *Nationwide*. I enjoyed every moment of every trip and took them all in my stride. Or did I?

The pace picked up again after the Christmas holidays and the trip to Lanzarote. All the things I love to do: filming, charity work, weekends with family. Fast forward to April, and I spent three delightful days in

Above: Commemorating
1916 in Boston.
Left: With Enya, filming
Christmas Carols from UCC.

A pre-Christmas trip
to London, with Dermot and Lucy.

Spain with friends followed by two days' work, then two days in Belfast with friends. The following week, Lucy and I were on that charity trip to Malawi, a wonderful insight into a pace of life that I respect so much more now than I did a year ago. I arrived home from Malawi at five thirty a.m. on a Friday, had a few hours' sleep and was in town later getting my hair colour done.

The following morning I was filming on the Shannon and returned to Dublin to be a guest, with Anne Cassin, on *The Ray D'Arcy Show* that night. Monday and Tuesday saw Anne and me recording *Nationwide* on the Waterford Greenway, and on Thursday morning at five thirty I was part of a group of twelve people flying to Belarus and Ukraine with Adi Roche to see the work of Chernobyl Children International. Home on Saturday, filming in Northern Ireland on Sunday, and that brought me into May, delighted as always to have been offered such rich opportunity in life, unaware that the pace had finally started to overwhelm me.

I've never been a great sleeper, but during May, my sleeplessness reached new heights or perhaps it plumbed new depths. Granted, the sun rises very early and the birds sing their hearts out, but my feelings of anxiety worried me while I lay there unable to sleep. I was waking at about three a.m., often bathed in perspiration, heart pounding and arms shaking. I sometimes wondered how I was going to get up and face the day. The number of hours stretching ahead of me and the number of tasks that had to be fulfilled were overwhelming.

This was so unusual for me. Previous summers had seen me waking early and jumping out of bed to go for an early-morning run as the sun rose. Even if my knees had not put paid to the running, I simply couldn't rise with enthusiasm, even on bright sunny mornings. I felt helpless, hopeless and, in some ways, useless. I distinctly remember one morning wishing I was in hospital because then I could stay in bed with tea and toast. John O'Donohue's poem 'Beannacht' kept coming into my mind.

> ' And so may a slow
> Wind work these words
> Of love around you,
> An invisible cloak
> To mind your life. '

I wanted somebody to mind me. Life seemed heavy, a struggle, and this feeling had been creeping up on me over the past few months. I kept going, though. I'm sure you're wondering why I didn't confide in anyone. The truth is, I wasn't sure what was wrong, and I was a bit ashamed of myself for feeling like that all the time. I have a great family, a stimulating job and a good social life. I should be counting my lucky stars, not feeling sorry for myself and overwhelmed.

In June I happened to visit my GP for an unrelated matter and toyed with the idea of bringing the subject up, especially when he asked me was there anything else. Just then I didn't know how to put words on how I was feeling. I hadn't fully identified the malaise and joined the dots. A few weeks later, though, I phoned my GP and outlined to him a shortness of breath that was starting to cause me alarm. I felt as if I was breathing from just below my chin and sometimes I'd draw a sharp quick breath, like a hiccup. As somebody who was sent to elocution lessons when I was a child, I knew that the correct and healthy way to breathe is to inhale and fill the lungs with air. I just could not do that, no matter how hard I tried, and I was worried as to why this should be.

This very patient and caring doctor listened as I explained, and asked me was I anxious about anything. Once again there was nothing I could put my finger on. He told me to relax, not to worry, not to stress myself. I didn't realise I was stressing myself at the time, but I was definitely below par. The words at the beginning of 'Beannacht' summed up my feelings about myself:

> 'On the day when
> The weight deadens
> On your shoulders
> And you stumble . . .'

I was stumbling from day to day until that morning, two weeks later, when I was loading the dishwasher and listening to Ryan on the radio in conversation with Róisín Agnew, journalist and magazine editor, about the blog she had written on her decision to change gear in her life. She was twenty-eight years of age and spoke of how her life in Dublin had got so busy that she felt overstretched, overwhelmed and underslept. She had lost any sense of pleasure in her achievements. Busyness had become a status symbol among her peers, some of whom were reluctant to take any holidays. When Róisín summed up her life as busy, lonely, tired and filled with anxiety, I realised I could tick those boxes. Her solution was to resign her job and take herself off to Portugal, where she works freelance at a pace she finds conducive to a much healthier work-life balance.

The phrase 'burnout syndrome' came up several times during that radio conversation, and that was my eureka moment. I made a few enquiries, read a bit about burnout, and saw it could well be the reason I was lacking motivation and enthusiasm. I had lost my chutzpah, my *joie de vivre*. I was summoning my resources for all of the different aspects of my life on the outside, but inside I was running on empty. This realisation made me feel very fragile, and I was emotional that whole day. The office was quiet because a number of people were on holidays, but one of my colleagues did ask me was there something wrong with my eyes because they were red. I put it down to having no make-up on. I don't know if she was convinced.

At the end of that day I resolved to make some changes in my life. I booked two weeks' holiday from work, even though I had no travel plans. That was a first because, since my children have grown up, I've taken a few days here and there to see different groups of friends, to catch up, to have a mini-break together. I was quite shocked by my children's reaction when I told them of my plans to take a fortnight off and not go away. They laughed and said I'd find it impossible to do nothing.

Out of the mouths of babes! I took a good hard look at myself and knew they were right. Free time for me meant doing the garden, the laundry, cooking, cleaning, shopping, ironing. When the lethargy crept in and I couldn't motivate myself to undertake all or any of those exciting endeavours, when I couldn't climb out from under the cloud, I felt guilt, a lack of achievement, lazy, useless.

Knowledge is power, though, and I took on board that I was doing too much, too fast, and that needed to change. I tackled the symptoms straight away. I was desperate, and would have stuck pins in my eyes if that had been recommended as part of the treatment. My life was a flat, grey, lifeless place, even though it was chock-a-block with running around doing stuff.

Some of the recommendations in the articles I read about Burnout Syndrome were easy to apply. For instance, I had developed the hugely common habit of checking my phone in bed before lights out. I'd set the alarm for the following morning, then have a quick look at Twitter and Instagram, check the news websites, see if any emails had arrived in the last while. It was not unusual for me to whittle away an hour or more like this. Eventually I'd put the phone down, then wonder why I couldn't sleep. Enough was enough.

I'm pleased to say it wasn't too difficult to break that habit. I set the alarm that very night and put the phone out of reach on the windowsill. I slept better than I had done for a long time. The phone was out of sight so Twitter and the like were out of mind. The phone came very sharply back to mind the following morning, though, when the alarm went off and I couldn't stretch out my hand to turn it off. I had no choice but to get up and go over to the windowsill. And I was up. I felt better about myself already. I knew there and then that I was not going to check my phone last thing at night ever again. And I haven't. It's just not worth it.

I felt so badly about myself last summer that I would have done anything to improve my sense of well-being. Turning off my phone was the first step and it wasn't much to ask for the difference it made.

Taking two weeks off work was a good move also,

and I understand now how important it is to slow down and not try to pack too much into a short space of time. I had actually forgotten some of the trips I had made from the start of last year and only remembered them when I looked at photographs. That is not good. I was viewing life as if it were an egg-timer, feeling it was important to experience as much as possible before the sand had fallen from the top to the bottom. That race-against-time mindset was a factor in my feeling of burnout. It had to go too. What's the point of embracing loads of experiences and travelling to different places if you hardly remember them or where you've been? I view that egg-timer differently now. It's about relishing the moment, being present to the people I'm with and, most importantly, being present to myself, not just racing hither and thither, getting a flavour of this or that.

I have made big changes in that area of my life: I take things at a slower pace and spend longer in places that I choose to visit. Eckhart Tolle, who wrote *The Power of Now* and is widely recognised for his spiritual writings and talks, hit the nail on the head when he said: 'I have lived with many Zen masters, all of them cats.'

You can see where he's coming from. Cats are serenity, calm, happiness all rolled into one. I'm actually looking at our cat, Maggie, as I write this. She's curled up and asleep in a shaft of sunlight in the conservatory. She'll wake in a while, stretch and continue her enjoyment of

Zen master Maggie, being photo-bombed by Daisy!

the day. I'm not suggesting we should or could live our lives like cats and do nothing but eat, sleep and stretch all day, but we can learn a lot from their calm, Zen-like demeanour.

I have changed the pace of my life and feel I'm enjoying it at a much deeper level. I work with enthusiasm and know that I'm lucky to be invited into people's lives, that it's a privilege to tell their story and share their optimism with *Nationwide* viewers. I rest much more. I used to see being on the go as a badge of honour. I've learned to pace myself, to say no to certain things and to undertake others with gusto. The poet Ovid, who lived from 43BC to about AD18 was an advocate of resting. He said, 'Take rest: the field that has rested gives a beautiful crop.'

Well, if Ovid could see the need for taking time out back in his day, can you imagine the need for rest, recuperation and recharging the batteries of our minds and souls in the frenetically paced world that we inhabit? So many of us take on too much and get burned out. I was that soldier, and the changes I have made in my life over the past twelve months have all been for the better. My 'beautiful crop' is the feeling that I can cope, that I am enjoying work, family, friends much more now because I'm not trying to fit everything into a small amount of time.

And, most importantly, I'm enjoying *me* more. That took a bit of getting used to. I, like many women, had got so used to putting the needs of everybody around me before my own that it felt very self-indulgent to be thinking of what I wanted or needed. It was a revelation to me that my children were relieved I was being more mindful of what I wanted or needed. They were delighted for me to be living life at a gentler pace, not trying to cram a week's activities into a day.

Mindfulness is an important part of my life. I am mindful of my need to pace myself, to embrace what I refer to as 'empty time', when I know, for instance, that there is work to be done but, if I don't feel like doing it, it will wait. I have trained myself to avert my gaze if I'm passing a bulging laundry basket, to resist the urge to do the ironing in case 'there's no time later on'. So what if there's no time later on and the ironing has to wait another day or week? *C'est la vie!* If I come home from work and want to sit and be still, that's what I do. It took me a while to be totally comfortable and guilt-free with that state of being, but it was worth the effort.

I believe it is very important for all of us, at every stage of life, to work hard at maintaining a balance between activity and stillness. As Charlotte Eriksson has written, 'Sometimes you need to sit lonely on the floor in a quiet room in order to hear your own voice and not let it drown in the noise of others.'

What can be more important than our own voice? We need to be mindful of ourselves, our needs, our desires. I do not want to get to the end of my life and reflect on the fact that I always tackled the ironing when the basket was full but would have liked to sit and contemplate my navel and didn't. The funny thing is that since I gave myself permission to relax and do nothing, I have noticed a renewed energy for the things I was failing to see the point of before I took myself in hand. My home has always been my castle and my sanctuary, but it was lacking a bit of TLC while I was falling into the trap of burnout. Now it's getting lots of hugs and kisses and is oozing love, warmth and welcome again.

Spirituality is also an important part of my life. Readers of my other books will know that I was brought up in a traditional Catholic home, where the Rosary was said every evening after tea. My mother went to seven a.m. mass every morning and we all went to confession on Saturdays and mass on Sundays. We fasted on Fridays, gave up sweets for Lent and took part in school retreats every year. I lived by the rules and it wasn't until I went to teach English in Brittany when I left college that I began to question certain aspects of Catholicism. French Catholics were not reared with the notion that non-attendance at mass was a sin. How could it be different for them? The man made rules of Catholicism started to unravel slightly for me with this simple observation. That coupled with subsequent horrible revelations of abuse within the church rocked me enormously and I became disillusioned with the institution. I abhor the way women are treated in the church and I cannot see the reason for compulsory celibacy. However I remain loyal to the religion into which I was born and I respect other people's loyalty to their own religions. When I'm visiting an African country I love to be woken early in the morning by the tinny sound on the tannoy of the Muslim call to prayer. And when I'm at home I like to hear the Angelus bells at noon and at 6 pm. I'm aware that there are people who would like to be rid of the bells that toll the Angelus in the interests of secularism. I think that would diminish the richness and variety of life in Ireland.

The Dalai Lama speaks wisely about different religious observances:

> 'All major religious traditions carry basically the same message, that is love, compassion and forgiveness ... the important thing is they should be part of our daily lives.'

We don't need to go to the chapel, the temple or the mosque to have those qualities as part of our daily lives but we do need to acknowledge that we have a spiritual aspect to our being, that is non-material, inner, emotional, caring. The word 'spiritual' comes from the Latin 'spiritus', which means breath. So we are talking life force here. I regret that in this increasingly secular and busy materialistic world in which we live the spiritual aspect of our lives doesn't get due recognition. Society is the poorer for it. When I was growing up in the fifties and sixties, murder and violent crime were big news because they so rarely happened. These days they are everyday occurences. I can understand people turning their back on organised religion. It has disappointed and been found wanting. Unfortunately, it hasn't been replaced in many people's lives and the vacuum has had regrettable consequences. We read of horribly violent random attacks and of lives destroyed. There is a hardness to life that is heartbreaking. There is a lack of kindness, compassion and love. Life is diminished where there is no recognition of the softer, gentler, caring qualities that are reflected in an awareness of our inner, spiritual being. The words of Buddha, who died in the fifth century BC, are just as relevant today as they were in ancient times.

‘Just as a candle cannot burn without fire,
men cannot live without a spiritual life.’

I nurture my spiritual life by going to mass, not every
Sunday but I do like being there and I particularly enjoy
mass in simple surroundings with friends. I pray, I light
candles, I visit graves and I feel very spiritually aware
when I spend time with my sister on the Aran Islands.

Deirdre has a wonderfully rich sense of the value of inner spiritual life force and she gives retreats in Celtic Spirituality. The beauty of creation is everywhere to be seen and enjoyed on Inis Mór. I revel in the simple pleasures of walking, climbing, and being in the unspoiled and majestic surroundings of such an ancient place, where my Irishness, my identity, is part of the ambience. I feel relaxed, renewed, positive, in control and happy when I spend time on the island. I value the antidote it provides to the demands of modern living and I appreciate its importance even more since

I experienced the horrors of burnout last year. In the words of the Indian spiritual master, Sai Baba:

> 'Man is lost and is wandering in a jungle
> where real values have no meaning.
> Real values can have meaning to man only
> when he steps onto the spiritual path,
> a path where negative values have no use.'

The present moment is the only one of which I can be sure. The sand in the egg-timer doesn't seem to be moving so fast from top to bottom, racing as it was before my eureka moment. It's travelling more slowly, and I'm savouring the moments it's counting out for me. That's not to say I don't have times of sadness and struggle. I do. I'm no different from anybody else. I live them and I know they will pass. I'm very glad, though, that the grey cloud of flatness has lifted and the feeling of being overwhelmed is under control. I'm so grateful to that radio interview of June last year, and I hope that anyone who is living in the dull flat way that I was experiencing will read this, take stock, research burnout and do their utmost to eradicate it from their lives. Then they can embark on a liberating, lighter journey from day to day.

I began this chapter with the comforting words of Hafiz about our hidden light and to end, here is his uplifting interpretation of the meaning of our lives:

'We have come into this exquisite world to experience ever and ever more deeply our divine courage, freedom and light.'

Hafiz, 14th-century Persian poet

Finding My Garden

"*In search of my mother's garden, I found my own.*"

Those words of the American author Alice Walker, best known for her Pulitzer Prize-winning novel *The Color Purple*, define quite clearly (for me) my lifelong interest in gardening. It crept up on me as I grew up in Clondalkin, in an ordinary semi-detached house with a driveway, a lawn, a skinny flowerbed under the sitting-room window to the front, and a slightly wider flowerbed, path and lawn at the back. That was my home, where my love of gardening was nurtured in simple, almost unconscious ways.

There was nothing fancy about our garden and, in fact, it was a struggle to achieve any successful planting, given the presence of two boys in our house and three cousins, all boys, living next door.

Our other next-door neighbours were the McCarthys, and a tall block wall separated our two houses. The height of the wall presented a challenge to my brothers and their cronies as they scaled the back walls from one end of the road to the other, running away from the guards, who had been called because they were playing football on the road and had kicked the ball into a neighbour's roses. Again! They would give each other a leg up, then fall to the grass on the other side, pick themselves up, dust themselves down (or not), and continue on their way. Once the escaping footballers had scaled the dizzy heights of the McCarthys' wall, they were like hurdlers at Santry stadium, flying through the remaining five gardens, whose walls were no more than waist high, to bring them to the end of the road and safety.

On the other side of our garden, the wall separating our house from our cousins' was of the lower variety, and there was a stile broken through it to facilitate easy access for my mother and her sister as they went from one house to the other every day for their tea after lunch.

When my brothers and cousins were not fleeing the law, they used the low dividing wall between our two

Cowboys and Indians — cousins, and a young Deirdre, in Brigid's Road, 1961.

houses as horses. Blankets or sheets would be thrown over it at intervals, a big stone carefully positioned at the front of each for the horses' heads and a rolled-up jumper did duty in the middle as a saddle. They would then run across the lawn, brandishing hurleys – sorry, rifles! – mount their steeds, assume the John Wayne position and head off in search of the Apache. On other occasions, they would be the Apache, which necessitated the erection of tents on the lawn. There was one tepee, which Santa had brought to my cousin Barry, that looked the part, but the others improvised with a few stakes shoved into the grass, rugs attached to the top and other paraphernalia.

The back garden also served as a pitch and putt course: my father and my uncle dug holes in the grass into which they sank empty baked-beans tins, and the tournaments commenced.

I recount these tales from my childhood memories to assure you that we did not have a fancy garden. It was trampled and pummelled by my two brothers, John and Tony, and my cousins, William, Brian and Barry. My sister Deirdre would join them on occasion, not running away from the guards, of course, but there are some cute photos in the family album of her and Barry sitting outside his tepee. I, being the eldest of them all and a nerd, was probably up in the back bedroom studying for my Primary Cert, a mistake definitely, a lost opportunity, but that was my disposition at the time. I certainly disproved the idiom that you can't put an old head on young shoulders.

I like to think I would have a more carefree attitude to life if I could turn back the clock. The boys certainly had lots of fun in the back garden and they recount some of the stories from those days to howls of laughter at family gatherings today. Our children gasp at the Neanderthal games and the improvisation associated with them, but they were happy times, and that sense of fun and freedom associated with home has stayed with all of us. For me home has to be an easy, relaxed place, where nobody stands on ceremony and everyone is welcome. I learned that from childhood days on St Brigid's Road, and I know that for John, Tony, William, Brian and Barry, those were happy times that now provide wonderful memories. Isn't that what any parent wants for their children?

My mother and Uncle Tom next door might have aspired to two colourful flower gardens, side by side in Clondalkin, but that's another matter. They tried but were thwarted by footballs, golf balls and marauding cowboys and Indians throughout their children's early years.

Our garden was well worn and well used by all the children on the road, yet certain aspects of it appealed to me from a very young age and, I think, sowed the seeds of my interest in gardening, one of the most satisfying, nurturing and pleasurable of pursuits.

The famous French artist Claude Monet, father of Impressionism, proclaimed, 'My garden is my most beautiful masterpiece.' This from the man who gave us such glorious paintings of lily ponds, poppies, poplars and the sunrise.

Although the flowerbed in the front garden was impossibly narrow, my mother planted hydrangeas in it, which didn't impress me much at the time but they are now one of my favourite plants: they are hardy, they flower abundantly and they look gorgeous in a jug on the kitchen table. Wasn't it the anarchist, political activist and writer Emma Goldman who said, 'I'd rather have roses on my table than diamonds around my neck'? I like roses on my table too but they are not as abundant as hydrangeas, in my garden anyway.

That narrow flowerbed was also home to a climbing pale pink tea rose, with a magnificent scent, positioned right beside the front door. Anybody standing in the porch waiting for the door to be opened was treated to its perfume. Now that's what I call a *céad míle fáilte*.

We are long gone from the family home. It was sold after my mother died in 2001, and, as I mentioned earlier, has been infused with new life by the young family who bought it. Although the new owners have modernised the front garden, they kept the scented climbing rose, which makes me very happy. Good call and good karma. They will never regret that decision.

Another delight, enjoyed in the early summer by passers-by, was a white lilac tree, planted just inside the garden wall. Out the back, as we referred to the back garden always, the flowerbed was most noted for trampled clay and not much else. It was difficult for flowers to survive the pitter-patter of thundering feet. There was another lilac at the bottom of the back garden, purple this time, and the centrepiece of the lawn was a cherry tree, which I could see from my bedroom window and adored for its pretty tissue-like blossom and the pink carpet on the grass when the blooms succumbed to the winds of early spring.

You understand by now that ours was a typically simple suburban garden, yet its few colours, perfumes and textures, courtesy of low-maintenance lilac, hydrangea, tea rose and blossom, formed an important part of the backdrop to my childhood and provided the spur for me to make a garden as soon as I had a house of my own.

Actually, I made a mini-garden even before I left home. My father was involved with Tidy Towns from 1958, when the competition was first held, and was an active member of the organisation in Clondalkin, which saw some success throughout the sixties. He must have seen the beginnings of a gardener in me: when I was eleven he encouraged me to enter the junior gardening competition organised by the local Tidy Towns committee. It involved digging a square patch of specific dimensions, planting it and tending it throughout the summer until the day of judgement arrived.

To that end, in the springtime of 1968, my mother's dressmaking measuring tape was laid across the flowerbed at the bottom of the back garden. The plot was measured and marked with a boundary of bamboo canes. I turned the soil diligently and, at intervals, planted packets of seeds, which by June would be a riot of colour to impress the judges. I remember distinctly planting sweet pea towards the back of my patch and, in a pattern of descending height, marigolds, pansies and whatever else was available in rows towards the front. The next job was to keep the birds away, which entailed making a hole in aluminium milk-bottle tops and attaching them to a piece of string. I hung it above my flowerbed, tied to the lilac tree at one end and a stone on the wall at the other. More of a threat than the birds, of course, were the cowboys, but my father summoned them and told them in no uncertain terms that my flowerbed was out of bounds for horses or fleeing the guards that summer. I can still see the sweet pea in my mind's eye, probably because I spent so many evenings wrapping the plants around stakes to keep them upright. If the judges weren't impressed by my other flowers I might win them over with the distinctive perfume of sweet pea. How could they resist?

Well, resist they did. The judges came unannounced

one Monday evening in July 1968, a date that is etched in my memory. I was in bed at the time and Mammy came running up the stairs to tell me they were out in the garden with Daddy, who, thankfully, had removed the line of bottle tops, which was effective but not aesthetically pleasing. I jumped out of bed, threw on a summer dress and flew down to the garden. A man and a woman, both of officious demeanour, were taking notes and measuring the patch. They hardly spoke, to me at any rate, and quite quickly they were gone.

The news was not good. Despite my diligent weeding and watering for months, I didn't win a prize. I was disappointed but undeterred. I continued to tend that patch for the rest of the summer and was particularly proud when I could offer my mother a bunch of sweet pea for the vase on the kitchen table. I had been bitten by the gardening bug, and it has been a source of satisfaction, peace, consolation and joy to me for more than fifty years now. I agree with the English artist Minnie Aumonier, who died in 1952. She wrote, 'When the world wearies and society fails to satisfy, there is always the garden.'

No matter how despondent, tired or lonely I feel, if I can get out into the garden and do a bit of watering, pruning, weeding or just pottering, it will be time well spent and I will feel better as a result. There's something about bending over, kneeling down, getting earth under your fingernails, clearing weeds, making space, adding colour, all physical and demanding activities, that has a grounding effect on the body and a calming effect on the mind. As May Sarton wrote:

'Everything that slows us down and forces
patience, everything that sets us back
into the slow circles of nature, is a help.
Gardening is an instrument of grace.'

When I got married and owned my first home, I was excited to plant a garden. My mother brought me to visit Miss Miller, her former boss in the College of Science, a tall, slender elderly lady who had a most magnificent garden in Glasnevin on the north side of the city. My mother had stopped working thirty years before this visit, because of the marriage bar, but she had maintained her friendship with Miss Miller who, as a single woman, continued to work in the civil service up to retirement age. All the while she was working she was developing a garden that would hold its own with the best of them, an oasis of colour and abundance at a Dublin suburban semi.

Although she was in her ninetieth year when I went to see her garden, she was as supple and strong as a woman half her age, because, as Rudyard Kipling reminds us, 'Gardens are not made by singing, "Oh, how beautiful," and sitting in the shade.' They demand a lot of physical work which, as well as being its own reward, improves fitness and flexibility. Miss Miller could attest to that. Following tea, scones and lots of gardening tips, she headed to the shed from which she emerged a few minutes later with a shovel and a fork. She proceeded to plunge them into the flowerbeds to dig up some 'slips', including a magnificent purple bearded iris, with a lovely old-fashioned perfume. I couldn't wait to get home to start planting.

That was thirty-five years ago, and the purple iris has been split and shared with lots of friends over the years. It has accompanied me to the two other houses I have lived in since that time. Miss Miller had introduced me to the practice of sharing plants, and to this day, as I'm walking around my garden, I remember the woman who gave me a slip from something in hers. I hope others do the same when they tend a plant that started as a slip from one of mine, a symbol of friendship, a connection, a reminder that, in the words of Antoine de Saint-Exupéry, author of *The Little Prince*, 'There is no hope of joy except in human relations.'

Gardening brings benefits even beyond those of beauty, personal well-being and a sharing connection between friends. I recently filmed a story for *Nationwide* at a Pavee Point and Irish Heart community garden in Finglas in Dublin, which is tended by Travellers in the area and was designed as part of a scheme to enhance the physical and mental health of those taking part. Traveller men were the main target group. It's shocking to discover that the suicide rate among Travellers is six times higher than it is in the rest of the population and seven times higher in the case of Traveller males.

This community garden is fulfilling a valuable function by offering those young men a purpose, a reason to get up in the morning, an opportunity to perform satisfying physical work and, most importantly, to see the fruits of their labour from what they plant, tend, watch grow and harvest. The success of the project is illustrated by the numbers of men who turn up day after day to

look after the garden. I asked them what their daily routine had been before the project had begun twelve months previously. The single men seemed to stay in bed till lunchtime, then 'hang around'. The married men brought children to school and hung around until it was time to pick them up. Each and every one of them felt that their lives were more meaningful since they got involved with the garden.

It was very moving to hear a young father say he loved his children being proud that he went to work every day. I was delighted for him. My heart went out to a tall, handsome, very shy nineteen-year-old, who hadn't missed a day at the garden since it opened. He had passed his Leaving Cert two years ago and had found it impossible to get any kind of job once his address became known to a prospective employer. His hope is that his experience in the garden will give him the skills to get farm work in the future. He loves working with the soil. The fact that some older Traveller women are also part of the gardening project has led to a positive inter-generational exchange. When it comes to gardening work, the women hold their own, but are also engaged in sharing their cooking skills with the men.

The day I was there, the vegetables were picked, brought to the kitchen, and the women showed the men how to make soup. While they had their undivided attention they added a class on making currant bread and plain soda bread. There wasn't a word of objection from the men. They followed instructions, and savoured the results of their work in the garden as they enjoyed the soup with fresh bread, straight from the oven, smothered in melting butter. This simple garden – on the grounds of a former detention centre for young offenders and made up of several raised beds, spilling over with cabbage, potatoes, runner beans, beetroot, rhubarb, strawberries and lots more – brought home to me yet again the value of gardening.

I know that gardening enhances my physical and mental well-being and my sense of peace and serenity. The community garden in Finglas has the added advantage of reaching out to a disadvantaged sector of our Irish brothers and sisters, and giving them a common purpose, a sense of belonging and the satisfaction of a job well done. In the words of English poet Alfred Austin:

> 'The glory of gardening: hands in the dirt,
> head in the sun, heart with nature.
> To nurture a garden is to feed not just
> the body, but the soul.'

The Circle of Life Garden epitomises for me the notion of nurturing the soul through gardening. It's in Salthill in Galway, a garden of commemoration and thanksgiving dedicated to organ donors, and is a labour of love by people who had the vision and drive to craft it. They are Denis and Martina Goggin, whose only child Éamonn died in a car crash in 2006 at the age of twenty-six and whose life and memory are the inspiration for the garden. Martina is a great gardener and Denis a gifted stonecutter. By combining their talents and enlisting an army of volunteers and donors, they have created an oasis of calm, a place of beauty and reflection, filled with imagery and symbolism that illustrates the spirit of giving and the enduring legacy of those who donate their organs. It's a place for families who have donated the organs of loved ones to remember that, alongside their heartbreaking loss and sadness, they have given life to another, with their generous act of organ donation.

The garden is welcoming and inclusive, designed for everybody who passes through its gates. It's situated across the road from the prom in Salthill. Galway City Council donated the Quincentennial Park to Strangeboat Foundation, set up by Martina, Denis and their supporters, to bring this project to fruition. If ever a garden deserved to be described as 'an oasis of calm and tranquillity', it's this one.

From the moment you walk through the gates of the Circle of Life Garden, you are brought on a journey of reflection, thanksgiving, remembrance and love, all centred around the theme of this life we hold so dear. You walk past five standing stones, arranged in a circle

Daisy

and beautifully carved to depict five stages on the journey of life. Hands are featured in each carving and they range from the Madonna cradling the baby, representing new life, to a hand holding a bird and its chicks in the sanctuary of the family and the home. My favourite is a carving of a currach, with an oarsman rowing, a wonderful representation of the journey of life, so fitting in this garden across the road from the sea.

As you continue, you pass along a wall of carved stones from national heritage sites in each of the thirty-two counties, representing donors from the whole of Ireland. There's a five-foot stone candle, sculpted from an old agricultural land roller, representing light, onto which is carved the Hippocratic symbol in honour of the medical staff who make donation and transplantation possible. This was sourced from Clonmacnoise on the river Shannon, which for centuries represented the spiritual heartland of Ireland.

Another favourite of mine is the font that came from the fourteenth-century St James Church, which stood on the grounds of what is now University Hospital, Galway (UHG). This was the hospital to which Éamonn was brought following his accident, where he died some days later, and where his parents took the decision to donate the organs of their beloved son. Éamonn's heart, kidneys and liver gave a second chance at life to four other people and this act of generosity in the face of grief was the inspiration for the Circle of Life Garden. When the hospital heard about the garden they offered Denis and Martina the font, which had been sitting in their grounds unused. It flows with water now and, as well as signifying the gift of life, is a reminder of the abiding connection between Martina, Denis and UHG, who cared for Éamonn in his last days.

As you proceed through the garden you come to the Global Heritage Walkway in the park behind the garden, which features stone from each of the five continents and communicates the global message of organ donation. Each of those stones has come from a site associated with a different aspect of the advancement of humanity. For instance, there's a piece from Groote Schuur in Cape Town, South Africa, where Dr Christian Barnaard performed the first heart transplant in 1966. Stone panels, with inspirational quotations, chosen by Martina, are dotted throughout the garden, a positive and uplifting accompaniment to any visit.

The backdrop to all of the artistic and symbolic stone features is a tapestry of colour and texture from beautiful flowers and shrubs. I told you Martina is a great gardener and this garden is a fitting tribute from her and Denis to their son, who died in his prime. They have put their hearts and souls into it. It's open all year round and is free to enter, with a donation box discreetly carved into the wall (I told you Denis was a master

stonecutter). Visitors can contribute to the upkeep of the garden and support the wonderful amenity that the Circle of Life provides and the important message of organ-donor awareness that it conveys.

This is one of my favourite public gardens in the country. I met Éamonn just once. In March 2006 I was filming an edition of *Nationwide* in Spiddal and had a cup of coffee with Martina. Éamonn came by and said hello. I remember him as tall, shy, gentle, with a warm and friendly smile. Martina introduced him to me and watched him lovingly as we chatted. Four months later, Éamonn was dead, his parents' lives changed for ever. They will grieve the loss of their son and his future always, but in the Circle of Life Garden, his memory lives on. This garden is visually beautiful, intellectually satisfying and stimulating, and nurturing the soul.

'I grow plants for many reasons: to please my eye or to please my soul, to challenge the elements or to challenge my patience, for novelty or for nostalgia, but mostly for the joy in seeing them grow.'

Those are the words of David Hobson. He was born in England but lives in Canada, and is well known as a gardening columnist, garden tour leader and entertaining speaker at horticultural societies and gardening clubs.

He is renowned for sharing his humour and passion as a lifelong gardener, and has his finger on the pulse when it comes to gardening, which he finds pleasing, challenging, nurturing and joyful. He forgot to mention the hard work! It's that too, but well worth it for the lift I get when I can sit in the garden and contemplate the results of my labours. Even if it's cold and raining, the grey of the day is offset by the view of my beloved garden from my kitchen window.

Mine is a normal suburban garden that I have enjoyed tending and enhancing since I moved into this house sixteen years ago. It's not posh. There's an imperfect lawn. I have yet to summon the energy to eradicate all the weeds in it. I don't mind, though. It looks lovely when it's cut and strimmed, and forms a nice foreground for the beds that are sectioned off by railway sleepers and overflowing with plants. I have six hydrangeas, the plant that keeps on giving, with big bright heads – they repay a regular drink of an ericaceous food by glowing in gratitude. There's a white hydrangea with a hint of green at the edge, a pink one, a white one and one that is half pink and half white. I don't know how that happened but it's a talking point when friends visit for the first time.

The planting is haphazard but rich in memories that come to mind as I weed, thin, water or feed. As I've said already, slips are precious for their association with the friends who provided them. There's Miss Miller's bearded iris, of course, and some other slips she gave me that day back in 1982, which I have brought with me as I moved house and embraced a new garden. I filmed twice for *Nationwide* in gardening author Helen Dillon's beautiful garden in Ranelagh and was in awe of her skill and exuberance with plants. I loved her *joie de vivre*. I suppose it's hard not to be of a joyous disposition when you're surrounded by such botanical beauties. Helen gave me slips from a couple of Peruvian Lilies, which I have tended diligently and which I am glad to say have multiplied and thrived. Phew! I would feel I'd let her down if they hadn't.

I really love the softly scented lily-of-the-valley that was a gift from my friend Bernie in Cork. It always reminds me of gift sets that women of my vintage regularly received as Christmas presents when we were a bit too old for toys but still young enough to want a present to unwrap. Those gift sets invariably included a lily-of-the-valley soap, and Bernie's slip brings me right back to when I would keep that precious soap for special occasions. For me, nostalgia that can be triggered so simply is part of the appeal of gardening. I can be alone pottering outside and feel connected to friends and happy occasions by a particular plant or a flower.

The American actress, fashion designer, socialite and keen gardener Lucy Douglas 'C. Z.' Guest wrote: 'I've

always felt that having a garden is like having a good and loyal friend.' It's reassuring to feel that you are never alone when you're enjoying the garden. And it's wonderful to spend time in it with friends and family. There's nothing I like more than to open the double doors from the kitchen and relax outdoors with a pal over a coffee, a glass of wine, or a barbecue.

Readers of my last book, *What Matters*, will know that my children gave me a wonderful sixtieth birthday present of decking. They bought it, cut it, laid it, and I loved it immediately. I appreciate it even more now, three years later, for the opportunities it has afforded us to get deeper into the heart of the garden.

By now you will have no doubt that home for me is a place of calm, security, peace and relaxation, and the decking has become an extension of those qualities and an integral part of my home. It reaches far enough down the garden to allow for a lounge area, with sofas and cushions, just outside the kitchen door and still leave enough space for a table and chairs, bordered on two sides now by flowerbeds.

The difference this has made to the way we experience the garden is enormous. Because the decking is off the ground, you can see from it all of the lovely planting and feel part of it rather than, as when you're on the path, just looking at it. The decking itself is a pretty colourful spot also. There is hardly a square inch that doesn't have a planter with summer bedding plants, surfinia and lobelia mixed together and cascading onto the wooden floor, overlooked by hanging baskets of trailing fuchsia, geranium, more surfinia and lobelia.

The initial planting is time-consuming in the early summer but after that is done the plants' needs are basic. It's really just a matter of keeping them fed and watered. A bit like us humans, really! I keep a big basin filled with water at the side of the house, and whenever I feel the underside of a hanging basket and realise it's a bit light, I plunge it into the basin, hold it down until it is totally submerged and no longer blowing bubbles, then leave it there overnight. I have devised a rota for the baskets and the smaller pots: as soon as one emerges from the basin, another takes its place and off I go about my business.

There's a handy hint for you. Watering a hanging basket in position is a fool's errand. It's impossible to give them enough unless you're lucky enough to have the time to water them every single day. A feed every ten days is a must also, as is the dead-heading if you want to have flowers blooming right through the summer and into the autumn. I take every chance I get to have my cuppa on the deck, enjoying the colour, the growth, the feeling of wellbeing that the outdoors gives me.

Is there anything nicer on a warm summer's night than having friends and family around for a meal in the back garden? A glass of bubbles, as we refer affectionately to Prosecco, or a beer with some nibbles in the soft seats, then a light and tasty supper at the patio table. I have electric lights and a water feature in the garden, but they have never worked properly, and the young electrician friend I've asked to fix them on so many occasions has spent hours and hours on them with limited success. They work for a few weeks and give up the ghost again. I have given up on them now, and I reckon if that poor electrician saw my number coming up on his phone, he'd run a mile. Life is too short to agonise over lights that don't work. I dot lanterns and candles around the garden where the lights should be shining, and they come into their own as the sun is setting.

There are those who might wonder about the frequency with which an evening in the garden can be enjoyed right through to darkness, given the propensity of Irish summer evenings to be pretty chilly, if not downright freezing, and with the possibility of rain never far away. I have those eventualities covered. I have a remote-controlled canopy, which, when activated, covers the deck very neatly. I know it was designed as a sunshade but this is Ireland and it's been worth every penny I spent on it for the shelter it has provided from rain.

There's something very nice about being able to hold firm when the showers come. No need to scurry for the conservatory, just hit the button and, hey presto, we're dry. Dry but cold, you might say. I have that covered also. I position throws and shawls over the backs of the sofas. I have electric heated lights that attach to the underside of the parasol on the patio table and a chiminea, which is a wonderful source of cheerful flames and heat as we sit around and chat into the night. We smell of campfire the next day, but that's immaterial. Nobody wears their best frock to a barbecue. The smell of wood is a homely reminder of a night spent outdoors in the company of good friends.

Those summer days of gardening and entertaining provide lovely memories to sustain me as the winter creeps in and the light fades. I am not an avid winter gardener although I have nicely shaped topiary that

comes into its own when the summer planting dies back and they stand tall and alone against the cream-coloured high walls. It's another fine vista from the kitchen window. The deck, though, is a pale reflection of its summer self. I remove the hanging baskets and confine myself to some winter flowering pansies and cyclamen in a few planters and pots.

The winter of Eva and Benny's wedding was an exception, though: I replaced the summer bedding in the baskets and every planter with white cyclamen and white pansies, so simple to do, magnificent in the run-up to the big day, and a big hit for the house party that followed when you would be forgiven for thinking I thought it was the middle of summer! The canopy was unfurled, two chimineas, one borrowed, were blazing, the lanterns were positioned all around the garden and the white flowers on the deck set the tone beautifully.

Gardening is a most undervalued aspect of our lives. How often have you heard somebody dismiss the notion of connecting with the soil by declaring that they are 'just not a gardener'? I believe gardening should be a compulsory part of schooling. The benefits are enormous, both physical and psychological. As Allan Armitage, professor of horticulture at the University of Georgia in the United States, reminds us: 'Gardening simply does not allow one to be mentally old, because too many hopes and dreams are yet to be realised.'

The hopes and dreams that were sown when I, as a child in Clondalkin, entered that Tidy Towns competition have brought enormous satisfaction right through my life. Gardening has been a reason for physical exertion, a consolation in times of sadness, a source of satisfaction when I see the fruits of my efforts. I value the connection I feel with the soil, the care it needs, the patience I need to plant, to tend, to watch and wait for flowering. I can safely say that the words of Alice Walker, with which I began this chapter, hold true for me. I went in search of my mother's garden and I have found my own. I have no lilac or cherry blossom but every time I tend my hydrangeas or treat my roses for black spot (I've already confessed to having limited success with roses), I think of my mother and her garden. She didn't have money for planters and bedding plants, even if they had been easily available in those days, but she loved the garden. She passed that love on to her eldest daughter, and I have only happy memories of her garden and any time I spent in it. My hope is that I, in my turn can pass that love on to my own children, and that they will look back on hours we spent together in our gardens as times of peace, rest, love and laughter.

They have seen the joy gardening has afforded me, and as they move away from the nest and establish their own homes, I can see that the gardening bug is biting them. They have yet to embrace the ongoing commitment and work of a successful garden, but they are starting to ask questions that I love to answer.

When Tom moved in with his girlfriend, Shona, and noticed 'dead-looking things' in a couple of planters on the balcony he consulted the oracle, his mother. On my advice, he started to water and feed them and was over the moon when, the following spring, they smiled up at him and emerged as living pink geraniums. He derived great satisfaction from breathing new life into them and restoring them to their former glory. The fact that Tom is also my grass-cutter means he has experienced the tedious side of gardening and endured it without complaint. This augurs well for a lifelong interest in gardening, and I've assured him he has years of happiness to look forward to with such an interest.

Francis Cabot Lowell, the father of the American textile industry, saw the value in gardening when he wrote:

> 'Gardeners instinctively know that flowers and plants are a continuum and that the wheel of garden history will always be coming full circle.'

Isn't that a nice thought? We expend our energy in the garden so that flowers will bloom and fill our souls with colour and warmth. We know they will die but we can relax in the knowledge that this beauty will return to our lives the following spring. For that we should be very grateful. Plants and flowers are indeed a continuum, and for me, they are inextricably linked with home.

If I lived in an apartment plants would feature just as prominently as they do here in my suburban house and garden. In an apartment I would take a leaf out of Tom's book and have planters on the balcony, full of life and colour, and if I didn't have a balcony, I would sacrifice a view from the window because the sill would be filled with plants reaching for the light.

I am happy that gardening is a part of my life: it enhances my sense of home and its meaning. The nineteenth-century British socialist, textile-maker and writer William Morris felt that you should 'Have nothing in your house that you do not know to be useful, or believe to be beautiful.'

Plants and flowers tick both boxes for me. They are pleasing to the eye, and they nurture my soul, particularly when I pick flowers from the garden and put them into a vase in the house. Now, that's continuum.

Running for Home

Man proposes, God disposes.

That's the title of a pretty graphic work of art, painted by Edwin Henry Landseer in 1846, depicting Sir John Franklin's failed expedition to the Arctic the previous year. Its wisdom and truth were brought home to me, full force, on St Patrick's Day this year. I had it all planned and was looking forward to a nice family day. Lucy was returning, very briefly, to Ireland after three weeks in New Zealand, Australia and Thailand, then heading out to the States two days later. My sister Deirdre was spending the weekend in Dublin and the rest of the family was around too. And Ireland was taking on England for the rugby Grand Slam that afternoon. What more could you want to make the day complete?

I had already got into the spirit of our national holiday by travelling to the Welsh valleys to record a *Nationwide* special from the village of Banwen, the homeplace, reputedly, of Patrick, from which he was taken by Irish invaders, who came in search of iron ore and took strong young men and boys back to Ireland as slaves. Not one of our proudest moments, perhaps, but it seems to have been the done thing at the time.

The rest is history, as they say. Patrick spent six years minding sheep, escaped, became a priest and returned to Ireland to bring Christianity to its people. All of this happened in the fifth century, which means the details are sketchy, but those bare facts correspond to what Patrick himself wrote in his *Confession*:

> 'My name is Patrick. I am a sinner, a simple country person, and the least of all believers. I am looked down upon by many. My father was Calpornius. He was a deacon; his father was Potitus, a priest who lived at Bannaven Taburniae. His home was near there, and that is where I was taken prisoner. I was about sixteen at the time.'

So there you have it, in the words of the man himself. Interesting to note that priests weren't subjected to the ridiculous rule of compulsory celibacy back in Patrick's time! I digress, though. That's a subject for another day. Back to Patrick. As the good people of Banwen Historical Society pointed out to us, the area was part of the Roman Empire in the fifth century, and the straight roads into and out of the village testify to that. You can almost imagine the chariots racing along at speed without having to worry about bends or corners.

About a thousand people live in the tiny village and they are very proud of their connection to St Patrick. They have erected a stone to mark the place of his birth, and the children in the local primary school write essays and sing about him in the run-up to the annual

St Patrick's Day parade. I felt a real connection to this valley, its people and its Welsh language, Cymraeg, through Patrick, and couldn't wait to get home to prepare for Lá Fhéile Pádraig.

My house was decorated appropriately, if not stylishly, with banners and bunting, a shamrock wreath, green candles and even a green, white and orange curly wig, which has seen better days, given that it was bought for the World Cup celebrations in 2002. You'll be glad to know that I binned it after this year's festivities. Or planned festivities. Remember the opening sentence of this chapter?

The day started well. Deirdre and I went to mass and sang our hearts out to 'Hail Glorious St Patrick'. We came home, had breakfast, lit the fire, lit the candles, made soup and guacamole (green avocado, white onion and orange-ish tomatoes). I collected Lucy from the airport and we sat down to lunch and the match. So far, so good. Excellent, in fact, given the result of the rugby match: Ireland saw off England in fine style, adding the Triple Crown and the Grand Slam to the Six Nations win, which was already in the bag. The house was warm, people were happy, and I felt very lucky to be surrounded by family at home.

We were invited to dinner at Tom and Shona's. Dessert was my contribution and I had everything ready to assemble an apple crumble. The forecast was for snow the next day so I decided to go for a jog in case the roads were hazardous on Sunday.

Four years ago I substituted fast walking for running. The knees had been giving me problems and I felt it was the correct thing to do 'at my age'. But I had been a runner since secondary school, through college days and ever since, fitting a jog into my routine most days and completing two Dublin City marathons, one in three hours twenty minutes and the second, nineteen years later, in four hours twenty minutes. I'm very proud of those achievements so the walking just didn't do it for me. It provided the same aerobic exercise, it maintained my weight and fitness, it was definitely kinder to my joints, but it didn't give me the buzz. Now, I wouldn't in any way compare myself to the legendary sprinter Jesse Owens (he won four gold medals at the Berlin Olympic Games in 1936) other than to say that I felt he was singing my song when he spoke about the joy of running:

> 'I always loved running … It was something you could do by yourself and under your own power. You could go in any direction, fast or slow as you wanted, fighting the wind if you felt like it, seeking out new sights just on the strength of your feet and the courage of your lungs.'

I missed the runner's high, and last summer I reverted to my old ways and started jogging again, three times a week, 4.8 kilometres each time. My Fitbit measures the distance covered, the calories burned and the steps taken! I reasoned with myself that, given my age and twenty-first-century life expectancy, my knees would see me out adequately and I could be seeking a worse 'high' than a nice run around the block. I recommend the feeling you get when you turn the key in the door, home after a 7.30 a.m. run. You are, quite literally, set up for the day. That's the way it worked for me, anyway, three mornings a week. As I mentioned earlier, that afternoon run on St Patrick's Day was an extra in case it snowed. I was getting in the first run of the following week in case I had to leave Dublin at cockcrow some mornings to go filming. Run number one would be in the bank, so to speak. Box ticked.

Readers of my previous books will remember that I like to recite the Rosary when I walk. It was a daily part of our household routine in Clondalkin when I was growing up. Back then I looked on it as a massive imposition and did everything in my power to distract my mother during teatime in the futile hope that she would forget and we would be spared the ten minutes on our knees facing into the bars of the kitchen chairs. More than ten minutes, actually, because she insisted on the trimmings to the Rosary as well.

Apart from frustrating our post-teatime plans, it didn't do me or my siblings any harm, and I think my mother would be delighted that on a long solo walk I enjoy the Rosary. I'm not sure she would approve of the intentions I attach to it, which can often be quite secular and contemporary! The Rosary is a bit of a mantra for me: the repetition is pleasant and comforting and reminds me of the security of home. Home thoughts from the heart, certainly. Its rhythm doesn't fit with the pace of a run, though, so it hasn't featured as part of my exercise routine much since last summer. More's the pity. I could have done with a bit of intercession during that fateful run on St Patrick's Day.

I am the master of controlled breathing during a run and I am convinced that is why I can run further than a lot of people without any effort. The formula consists of breathing in for eight seconds, then out for eight. Continue at that rate for as long as you can. Then reduce it to six in, six out, then four, three, and the end point should be in sight by the time you're down to two seconds in and two seconds out – or gasping for air as the case may be. Try it. It works. You can keep going for much longer than if you start off breathing normally. Correct breathing technique is so important for running. Remember what the American writer Erma Bombeck said about it: 'The only reason I would take up jogging is so that I could hear heavy breathing again.'

There's heavy breathing for sure during a run, but I'm not sure it's quite the kind that Erma had in mind! In her day she was a very funny columnist and wrote a string of bestselling insightful books on domesticity. Titles like *I Lost Everything in the Post-Natal Depression*. Another of her books is *Motherhood: The Second Oldest Profession*, and how about *Family – The Ties That Bind … and Gag!* Are you recognising a common thread here? Maybe she should have given the jogging a chance!

Back to my measured run on Saturday, 17 March. Breathing in and out, thinking nice thoughts, enjoying the fresh air, planning ahead to having a shower, making an apple crumble and heading out to dinner when, all of a sudden and without any warning, I found myself face down on the pavement. I had fallen. The ground was dry, the surface even. This was the same route I ran every time and yet, for some reason, I fell. I don't know if there is anybody who enjoys running, or walking even, who hasn't stumbled at some stage. Sometimes you manage to avoid falling, at other times, after three or four awkward steps, you hit the deck but it's a gentle descent, if humbling nonetheless. You pick yourself up, dust yourself down and start all over again.

Not this time. I went from upright to face down in zero seconds. Knees, wrists and full-on face on the gravel. In time-honoured fashion, I picked myself up

immediately. I covered my mouth and walked the rest of the way home. My knees and hands were stinging, my nose hurt and my teeth had taken a bit of a knock but I felt okay. When I put the key in the door and looked in the mirror, I could see a scratch on my nose. The relief was enormous. I was home. I had reached the safe harbour, a bit shaken but it could have been a lot worse.

As it happens, it *was* a lot worse. When I took my gloved hand away from my mouth, it was covered with blood. I looked down and my cream tracksuit top was also bloodied. I knew I was in trouble. I remained remarkably calm for somebody who panics at the sight of blood. I called my sister, telling her I'd fallen.

When she came out of the sitting room, she had a more complete view of the damage than I did because she could see the blood streaming down my tracksuit top. Deirdre wouldn't be a fan of blood either: I only found out two days later that, although she put ice in a towel and placed it on my mouth, she didn't actually look at the afflicted area. This admission prompted me to ask her what she had intended doing therefore with the Steri-Strips she'd found in the first-aid basket upstairs. She said she was going to stick them on without looking. I'm so glad I insisted on going to the Swiftcare clinic!

A few hours later, I left the clinic with six stitches in my chin, a swollen lower lip that I thought was going to explode and the beginnings of a bruise below the lip that only fully came into its own the following day. I wasn't black and blue. My face was just plain black. It was disgusting and frightening, and I felt vulnerable and shaky for a long time afterwards. I was out of work for two weeks. I don't think the loyal viewers of *Nationwide* would have remained loyal if they'd been subjected to my presence on their screens.

In any event, I wasn't up to it. My confidence had taken a battering. I would wake up at night shaking. I was emotional and teary for no reason. I couldn't bear thinking about what had happened that day, yet I found my thoughts wandering back there if I let them. I didn't want to go outside the door. I hated looking in the mirror. I doubted that the bruising would disappear completely and that the scarring would lessen. I could see my situation in Edwin Landseer's painting of Franklin's wrecked ship being ravaged by polar bears. *Man proposes, God disposes*. I was nervous, anxious and frightened.

What shook me most, though, was that I wanted my mother. It really undermined my sense of self-worth. I'm a grown woman with four adult children, and my mother has been dead for seventeen years. I have worked hard and achieved success in various aspects of my life. And yet, following that minor accident while out for a run, I needed my mother. I railed against it. I felt I had to pull myself together or I might as well just throw in the towel. Now, with the vision of hindsight and having recovered from that horrible event, I can accept that I felt that need. It was tied up in my healing process.

My mother was the pivot of the home and of my life as I was growing up. She epitomised security, safety and hope, all of which I needed badly as I came to terms with the fall and its consequences. I have spoken to other people, some of whom have endured much worse pain and hardship than I, some less. All agree that when the chips are down, those of us who are lucky enough to have had a secure and safe home life revert to the comfort of those childhood days. My sincere wish is that my children, when and if the need arises, will find solace in thoughts and memories of home and that I will be there to provide that comfort and ease their pain. My mother would have wished that for me and for her other children.

After that fall in March, I felt very conscious of my age and questioned whether I was taking too many chances with my health by continuing to run. The shock of the impact took a long time to wane, and if I had a euro for every time somebody reminded me that we get more awkward on our feet as we age, I would be a wealthy woman now. Maybe it was time to slow down and stick with the walking. I can't believe I'm actually writing those words, which would have been totally alien to me before the fall but they were at the forefront of my consciousness for quite a while afterwards. I couldn't bear the prospect of something like that happening to me again. I lost my courage. The lines from the prose poem 'Youth', by the American writer and humanitarian Samuel Ullman, ring very true for me:

'You are as young as your self-confidence, as
    old as your fears;
  as young as your hope, as old as your despair.'

My physical recovery took two weeks, but the emotional and psychological injury took a lot longer to heal. I questioned my ability to do my job. How could I summon the enthusiasm to meet people and share their stories for *Nationwide* when I was feeling tired and bruised within? I had been looking forward to a holiday abroad, which had been booked since Christmas and was due to begin three weeks after the fall: suddenly its appeal was fading. I felt guilty to be going away so soon after I had been off work sick for two weeks. When I voiced those feelings, I was reassured by friends, colleagues and family that a holiday would be just the thing in the circumstances and that I should go off and enjoy it.

To be honest, that is exactly the advice I would give somebody else, but *I* couldn't feel it. My mind was tumbling with negative thoughts and concerns, and I spent many restless nights, toing and froing, during those dark hours of the mind and the soul. I felt vulnerable, alone, fearful and old. Ullman's words were never far from my thoughts and I worried that despair would follow before long:

> '	Nobody grows old merely by a number of years.
> We grow old by deserting our ideals.
> Years may wrinkle the skin,
> but to give up enthusiasm wrinkles the soul.
> Worry, fear, self-distrust
> Bows the heart and
> turns the spirit back to dust.'

That poem was a favourite of General Douglas MacArthur and he kept a copy of it pinned to the wall of his office in Tokyo when he became Supreme Allied Commander in August 1945. He often quoted from it in his speeches, and because of that it became better known in Japan than it was in the United States.

By coincidence, the holiday I embarked on following my fall was to Japan's Asian neighbour, China, and the two weeks I spent there went a long way to restoring

my equilibrium, my confidence and my sense of self. I appreciate now that time out is very important after a body shock. I had time to think, to acknowledge my weakness and gather my resources again. I had time to harness my energy and to observe that very different cultural space.

I was impressed by the Chinese people's can-do attitude, their pragmatism, their ability to let things go and get on with life. I saw old women pushing rickety bikes, laden with cardboard, to the recycling centres, where they would receive a pittance for their efforts. I saw people sitting on the kerb for hours on end, selling vegetables and dried fish, being jostled, ignored, stepped over. I saw people exercising in the parks at first light on their way to work. I saw people laughing and having fun. These are a hardy people. They restored my faith in the resilience of the human spirit and in my ability to pick up the pieces of my life and live it to the full. I returned from China full of vigour, enthused to get back on the horse, so to speak, to move onwards and upwards and put the fall behind me. As Samuel Ullman wrote:

> ❛Youth means a temperamental predominance of courage over timidity of the appetite, for adventure over the love of ease.❜

People will remember 2018 for the Beast from the East snowfalls and, just when we thought spring had sprung, the arrival of the Son of the Beast. They will revel in the memories of a glorious summer. They will speak of Ireland's magnificent third Grand Slam win that same year, and when St Patrick's Day is mentioned, I will remember the Latin phrase '*Homo proponit, sed Deus disponit*' from Book One of *The Imitation of Christ*, the English translation of which begins this chapter.

What happened that day was a reminder that life turns on a sixpence: things change without any warning whatsoever. I never got to make that apple crumble; my confidence as well as my face took a hammering and it took me a while to recover. Recover I did, though, galvanised in my intention to make the most of what I hold dear: family, friends, home, colleagues, projects and time spent with all of these.

Maya Angelou wrote:

> 'I can be changed by what happens to me
> but I refuse to be reduced by it.'

That fall was a reminder that I must live my best life now. I want to be present to those I hold dear. I want my home to be a place of love and comfort to all who come through its doors. I want my heart to be open to positive thoughts, to accept that life is precious, that relationships are what matter and that home is a sanctuary, a place where pain can be shared, wounds can be touched with a tender hand, where healing happens and recovery is assured.

> 'Our sorrows and wounds are healed
> only when we touch them with compassion.'
>
> Buddha.

Acknowledgements

Heartfelt thanks to everyone who has helped me during this writing adventure. Thanks to my editor Ciara Considine, to Breda and all the very supportive team at Hachette Ireland. Photographs have a special place in this book. Thanks to Kerry Kennelly from *Kerry's Eye* for permission to use the very moving photos he took during our trip to Vesnova with Chernobyl Children International. Thanks to David McClelland for the beautiful photos of Eva and Benny's wedding, to Joanne Murphy for the "good enough to eat" photos of the recipes and special thanks and love to my daughter Lucy Foster for the photos she took in Malawi and also at home in our garden. I am especially proud that she was the photographer for the cover shot of me (and Daisy of course!).

Thank you Neven Maguire for being such a good friend and for the delicious brown bread recipe which is a staple in my home. Thanks to the family of the late John O'Donohue for permission to quote from his very beautiful poem 'Beannacht'. Sincere thanks to my children, my dear friends, relatives and neighbours who fill my heart and my home with love and laughter. Finally and most importantly, heartfelt thanks to my late parents, Tom and Pauline, for the safe, secure and loving home they provided for me, John, Deirdre and Tony.

The publisher would like to thank Random House Group Ltd for kind permission to reproduce a passage from 'Beannacht', from *Anam Cara: A Book of Celtic Wisdom* by John O'Donohue, published by Bantam Press.